UPLIFTING
LEADERSHIP

UPLIFTING LEADERSHIP

HOW ORGANIZATIONS, TEAMS, AND COMMUNITIES RAISE PERFORMANCE

Andy Hargreaves,
Alan Boyle,
Alma Harris

JB JOSSEY-BASS™
A Wiley Brand

Published by Jossey-Bass
A Wiley Brand
One Montgomery Street, Suite 1200, San Francisco, CA 94104-4594—www.josseybass.com

Jossey-Bass books and products are available through most bookstores. To contact Jossey-Bass
directly call our Customer Care Department within the U.S. at 800-956-7739, outside the U.S.
at 317-572-3986, or fax 317-572-4002.

Wiley publishes in a variety of print and electronic formats and by print-on-demand. Some
material included with standard print versions of this book may not be included in e-books or in
print-on-demand. If this book refers to media such as a CD or DVD that is not included in the
version you purchased, you may download this material at http://booksupport.wiley.com. For more
information about Wiley products, visit www.wiley.com.

Library of Congress Cataloging-in-Publication Data

Hargreaves, Andy.
    Uplifting leadership : how organizations, teams, and communities raise performance / Andy
Hargreaves, Alan Boyle, Alma Harris.
        1 online resource.
    Includes index.
    Description based on print version record and CIP data provided by publisher; resource not
viewed.
        ISBN 978-1-118-92133-3 (pdf), ISBN 978-1-118-92134-0 (epub),
        ISBN 978-1-118-92132-6 (hardback)
        1. Leadership. 2. Organizational effectiveness.   I. Boyle, Alan, 1945–
II. Harris, Alma, 1958– III. Title.
HD57.7
658.4'092—dc23
                                                                              2014014578

Printed in the United States of America

FIRST EDITION

HB Printing 10 9 8 7 6 5 4 3 2 1

To our Mums and Dads who raised us.

Contents

Introduction: Uplift   1

1   Dreaming with Determination   17
2   Creativity and Counter-Flow   45
3   Collaboration with Competition   67
4   Pushing and Pulling   93
5   Measuring with Meaning   113
6   Sustainable Success   137
7   Uplifting Action   159

Appendix: Research Methodology   *177*
Notes   *181*
Acknowledgments   *207*
The Authors   *209*
Index   *213*

UPLIFTING
LEADERSHIP

Introduction: Uplift

The greater danger for most of us lies not in setting our aim too high and falling short; but in setting our aim too low and achieving our mark.
—Michelangelo

How does a giant multinational company turn itself around after seventeen straight quarters in the red? What does it take to transform a tiny developing country into a global economic powerhouse within a single generation? How can you be a top sports team when you're choosing from the smallest pool of players and have fewer resources than all your competitors? How do you do a lot with a little, create something from almost nothing, and turn failure into success?

These are the kinds of challenges we uncovered and questions to which we found answers when we studied fifteen organizations and systems in business, sports, and public education between 2007 and 2012. We set out to discover how each of these groups dramatically improved their performance against unfavorable and even overwhelming odds. Eventually, after analyzing hundreds of interviews, and writing thousands of pages of case reports, the answer came down to one word: **uplift**.

In aerodynamics, uplift is the force created by airflow, momentum, and wing design that enables large birds or huge aircraft to take off against gravity. Among people and within organizations, uplift is the force that raises our performance, our spirits, and our communities to attain higher purposes and reach unexpected levels of achievement. This book is about uplift, its effect on performance, and the ways to achieve it. It's a little word that makes a big impact.

"Up" is one of the first words we respond to when we are babies. We hear it spoken with a raised pitch. We lift up our eyes and stretch out our arms. Two letters. One syllable. *Up*.

Up is a direction, the way to get to a place we want to be. It pulls and invites us towards our destination. It is as viscerally inviting as the very first times we heard it when our parents lifted us into their arms.

"Up" is more of a *process* than a state. If you feel "up" about something, you are being optimistic. If you are "picking up" after an illness, you are starting to improve. We use "up" when we want to express that we're *making progress* towards our desired state— even though we haven't quite arrived.

Being "up" isn't always positive, of course; you can be uprooted, experience upheaval, or feel upset. But in general, it's better to be up rather than down. If you're up, starting up, or moving up, you are usually headed in the right direction, and you're definitely further along than you used to be.

Uplift has three interlocking meanings that are concerned with emotional and spiritual engagement, social and moral justice, and improved performance in work and life. Let's look at each of these.

Emotional and Spiritual Uplift

Being up is one thing. Getting up is another. It takes effort. The force that moves or holds us up is "lift." Authors Ryan and Robert Quinn describe lift as the "force that pushes a solid body upwards through the air."[1] The inspiration for their book, *Lift*, is the pioneering contribution to early aviation of Orville and Wilbur Wright. The Quinns explain that before the Wright Brothers famously launched their first manpowered flight from Kitty Hawk in North Carolina in 1901, they built a wind tunnel out of a soap-box to measure the effects of wing design and wind-speed variation on the relative impact of the forces of lift and drag—two forces that their German predecessor Otto Lilienthal had first identified in his ultimately fatal experiments with gliding. The Wright brothers concluded that in order to achieve successful lift in flight, you need the right kinds and combinations of forward motion, currents of air, and a navigation system of wing technology and steering controls. These forces, Ryan and Robert Quinn argue, apply not only to physics but also to personal and organizational change as well.

Often in human relationships, we can get an emotional or spiritual lift. At times like this, we say that we feel "uplifted." Powers of levitation and ascension are central to Buddhist, Hindu, and Christian theology. Great myths and true stories have the same effect when they describe people who have overcome adversity, survived ordeals, dramatically turned their lives around, or sacrificed themselves for the sake of others. People felt uplifted by Mother Theresa's actions to give her life to destitute children of India's slums, and by Nelson Mandela's forgiveness of the enemies who had imprisoned him on Robben Island. By enabling us to empathize with other people's example, such stories about acts of courage, humility, and selflessness inspire extraordinary effort in ourselves.

Uplifting actions and words are infectious; their effects spread out and influence others. We uplift others when we uplift ourselves, and vice versa. We lift each other's spirits, raise each other up to higher moral ground, and surpass ourselves.

Emotional and spiritual uplift is the beating heart of effective leadership. It raises people's hopes, stirs up their passions, and stimulates their intellect and imagination. It inspires them to try harder, transform what they do, reach for a higher purpose, and be resolute and resilient when opposing forces threaten to defeat them. Uplifting leadership makes spirits soar and pulses quicken in a collective quest to achieve a greater good for every-one, because we feel drawn to a higher place as well as to the people around us as we strive to reach it.

Social and Community Uplift

"Up" says things not only about our emotional state, but also about our power and status. If we go upmarket, we are appealing to higher-status customers. Uprisings can overthrow oppressive regimes. And upward mobility improves people's opportunities and life chances.

The idea of uplift has been a driving force of struggle and improvement within African American communities for more than 150 years.[2] "All labor that uplifts humanity," Martin Luther King Jr. told us, "has dignity and importance and should be undertaken with painstaking excellence."[3] More recently, Barack Obama has written about how he was lifted up from his surround-ing circumstances when he attended a magnet school. He in turn now endeavors to uplift the American people as their president.[4] Uplift is a collective force that leaders create together to raise everyone's prospects—especially those with the least advantages.

Uplifting Performance

Uplift's emotional, spiritual, and collective social powers mean that it also has the power to **improve people's performance and results**. It makes individuals and organizations do better than they had before, helps them to outperform their opponents, and inspires them to succeed despite meager resources. Uplift enables people to take off and then stay aloft. The way they achieve this is through *uplifting leadership*.

Uplifting leadership raises performance by creating spiri-tual, emotional, and moral uplift throughout an organization and among the wider community that it influences. It draws on and uses many of the "soft" processes or skills that have made a comeback in business in recent years.[5] Countless sources tell us that sustained high performance comes from focusing more on values than on profits.[6] Great companies encourage exceptional performance when they inspire a driving passion for the work that their people do.[7] Enduring success occurs when we feel that our work is creating emotional and social value—not just financial returns.[8] Employees want their organizations to stand for something important, to contribute to something that is worthwhile, and to improve people's quality and experience of life.[9]

Improved performance doesn't just come as a result of a focus on "soft processes," though. It's not just about wishing and hoping, or even about having more emotional intelligence or giving better support. This doesn't mean that the pursuit of excellence should be hard-nosed, callous, or cynical, either. But we can only realize high performance through hard work. Businesses that go bankrupt ultimately create no social value for anyone. And if people are going to achieve their dreams, they will need perspiration as well as inspiration.

Combining "soft skills" and hard work is central to sustainable success—not only in the corporate world, but in public services too. Indeed, the public sector offers some of the best examples of soft skills around—not surprising, perhaps, given that this is where some of the best women leaders are to be found. In public education, for example, schools that succeed in the face of overwhelming odds inspire their teachers and students with bold visions and also set impressively high expectations for everyone involved.[10] Though leaders in this field insist upon relentless dedication, they know that it cannot come at the expense of burning people out. There is great pressure on everyone to improve, but there is also constant support for the adults in the school to bring out the best in their students. When whole systems with hundreds of individual schools succeed despite their challenging circumstances—and manage to do so over many years, not just one or two—this is because they bring together what other people too often drive apart—pressure and support, passion and performance, the insatiable desire to learn along with the uncompromising demand for success.[11]

Investigating Uplift

We have more than a few clues, then, about the different factors that produce sustained high performance, especially in circumstances where we might least expect it. But there has been little firsthand investigation of what these factors look like across very *different* sectors, or of what it is that holds them together.

This is what our book sets out to do: to explain and exemplify the actual practice of what we call *uplifting leadership* from our seven-year study of fifteen organizations in business, sports, and public education in eight countries across four continents. Details of our multiple case-study methodology are presented in the Appendix.

Our original research question was: *"What characteristics make organizations of different types successful and sustainable, far beyond expectations?"*

The cases included in this book had to meet two or more criteria for performing above expectations:

- They **did considerably more with less** in terms of having relatively weak investment, experiencing limited resource capacity, or encountering very challenging circumstances.
- They performed **better than they had previously.**
- They performed **better than similar organizations** or systems.

We concentrated on analyzing organizations and systems that had done a lot with a little, could create something from almost nothing, or had turned failure into success. We also did our best to ensure that none of our cases had obvious records of unethical performance in the way they treated workers, clients, and the community. Indeed, we rejected cases where there was disregard for environmental responsibility in business, lavish spending on players to boost success in sports, or statistically questionable manipulation of achievement data in education.

The organizations we studied had been performing well for some time when we investigated them. But we know that high performance is not a permanent state, even for those at the very top of their game. The performance of many of the "excellent" companies identified by Peters and Waterman, for example, later plummeted—some of them quite quickly.[12] And in *How the Mighty Fall*, Jim Collins acknowledged that a number of the outstanding companies he had identified in his previous books had not endured.[13]

Our own work is about enduring achievement, not everlasting success. Many businesses suffered to some degree or other during the global economic collapse of the past few years, and our business cases too were among some of these. One or two of the sports teams fell back a little after our study was completed, though they rebounded again just as quickly later on. Although the high performers in public education have been the most impressive in maintaining long-term success, even they have not been immune to changes in the systems within which they have had to operate.

Analysis of our extensive database on sustained high performance beyond expectations condensed around six factors of uplift and uplifting leadership that together make up a kind of journey in which all of them play equally significant roles.

What Uplifting Leadership Is NOT

Before we introduce these six factors of uplifting leadership, it's important to be clear what uplifting leadership is *not*. Many all-too-common approaches to improvement and turnaround actually drag people down rather than elevating them to higher levels of performance.

First, uplifting organizations and their leaders in our study **didn't make it their goal to be at the top**. It wasn't their sole purpose to be Number 1, top of their league, or even best in class for their own sake. They were not driven by how high they wanted to go, or what rank they could achieve as their overriding purpose. Interestingly, the nations that have ranked among the highest on international tests of student achievement, such as Singapore, Finland, and Canada, didn't get there by *wanting* to be Number 1, or even in the top five.[14]

Second, uplifting organizations and their leaders **didn't follow others to the top**. They weren't merely imitating the practices of those organizations that made it there before them, by following the paths they had already taken or by borrowing the strategies that they deployed. Indeed, if you follow the path that others have taken, it is unlikely you will get any further ahead than they have.

Third, uplifting organizations and their leaders **didn't concentrate solely on hitting every milestone along the way**. They didn't just set targets and define Key Performance Indicators (KPIs) that their people were required to meet, in order to reach every milestone on the way, on time, and on target. Yes, KPIs can often help team members to attain high performance; however, when they feel under excess pressure to meet these KPIs in situations where goals are unclear or the consequences of failing are punitive, people typically adopt self-defeating practices driven by fear of failure rather than ambitions for success. In business, this often results in focusing efforts on quarterly returns at the expense of long-term strategy.[15] In education, it leads to narrowing the curriculum and constantly preparing children for tests, rather than actually teaching them *how to learn*.[16]

Fourth, uplifting organizations and their leaders **didn't push people to the limit** to deliver results in line with imposed targets. They didn't place undue reliance on relentless top-down pressure to hold people accountable for their desired outcomes. They knew that too much top-down pressure as well as insufficient bottom-up support would hold people down rather than lifting them up.

Last, uplifting organizations **didn't race to the top as quickly as possible** in a feverish attempt to "beat out" everybody else.[17] Indeed, those who adopt this fast-track strategy find that they expend all their resources too quickly, and wear people out before attaining their goal.

Uplifting Leadership

So, if uplifting organizations and their leaders didn't aim to be top, race to the top, drive people on towards the top, set milestones that people had to reach on the way to the top, or try to get to the top by following others' paths—what *did* they do?

What the organizations and leaders we studied *did* do was to engage in a process of uplifting leadership involving six interrelated factors that compose a journey to improbable success. Each of these factors also exhibits some inner tensions between what people conventionally consider to be "soft" and "hard" parts of leadership and management—tensions that uplifting leadership welcomes and capitalizes upon, rather than avoids or eliminates.

Together, these combined factors create the process of Uplifting Leadership as illustrated in Figure I.1. They also make up the framework of the next six chapters. They are

- Dreaming with Determination
- Creativity and Counter-Flow
- Collaboration with Competition
- Pushing and Pulling
- Measuring with Meaning
- Sustainable Success

Figure I.1   Uplifting Leadership

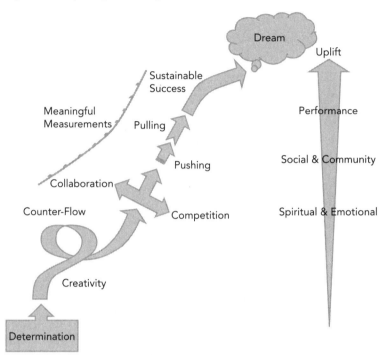

We outline each factor before going into detail in the following chapters.

1. Dreaming with Determination

The journey of uplifting leadership begins by defining a clear and compelling **"dream" or destination**—and determining how we'll get there from an unwanted or underestimated departure point. This destination also resonates with or revives people's sense of their own best identity. The process requires that we set out for a distant and improbably fantastic destination from a lowly, unlikely, and even stigmatized starting point. It is a compelling journey, necessitated by a moral imperative that is greater than anyone undertaking it—to support or even save the community they serve, or to create something of new or greater value that did not exist before. In this courageous and committed quest, destiny and destinations are connected to what people feel part of, to where they have come from, and to the best of what they have been before. Later, we will see how the incoming CEO of UK-based retail giant Marks & Spencer (M&S) reminded his workforce of the company's historic commitment to quality, price, and value, while becoming a leader in environmental sustainability. This is more than merely rebranding; it's about making a coherent connection between a motivating future and a well-remembered past.

In uplifting leadership, the dream is worth fighting for, and pursuing it is a matter of resolution and persistence as well as imagination and inspiration. Doing so builds momentum and helps ensure the effort does not fall short of the mark. In the quest to achieve and sustain high performance far above normal expectations, progress is typically uneven, adversity is abundant, and obstacles or even enemies have to be surmounted and surpassed. But the memory or prospect of failure is a constant force that deters backsliding and fuels determination to keep on moving forward to fight for a higher purpose rather than taking flight from the fray. Failure is not fated. Rather, it fuels the determination to keep forging ahead. We will see examples of companies who had to fight off rivals in order to reach extraordinary levels of performance—just as global auto-manufacturing giant Fiat Auto is constantly challenged to do. You may even need to take on opponents as formidable as the Terminator in order to secure justice for the children in the state where he is your governor. But the battle is more of a moral fight for what you believe in than a fight to kill off opposition for its own sake.

2. Creativity and Counter-Flow

Uplifting leadership forges **creative pathways** to reach the desired destination. You won't always be able to take the easiest or most obvious path. In part, creativity consists of flair, fantasy, and playful speculation about alternate possibilities to what already exists.

But the creativity of uplifting leaders is also counterintuitive. It goes against the flow at the risk of provoking doubt and derision. Uplifting leaders see opportunities that their competitors miss. They use opposing forces to their advantage. They do not follow in others' slipstream, but head into the wind to force a change of direction. Dogfish Head Craft Brewery began by putting ingredients in its ales that were inconceivable in mainstream beers; yet it is now one of the most successful independent breweries in the United States. Later, we will see how this success has come about not just from having unusual ingredients, but also from building a culture among the employees that is just more "fun" and "funky" than comparable competitors.

3. Collaboration with Competition

Part of the counterintuitive approach to uplifting leadership is to collaborate and combine with actual and potential competitors. Leaders and members of uplifting organizations know that competition and collaboration are not mutually exclusive alternatives, but coexist in unlikely combinations. Competition is the driving force behind most team sports, and is particularly intense in the sports-crazed nation of Australia. Yet, as we will show in this book, Australia's national organization for its top sport—cricket—took a business idea from two professors from Harvard and Yale to collaborate with their biggest competitors for financial advantage. We will also see how a private nonprofit company, The Learning Trust, changed the worst school district in England from being an educational no-go zone into a high-achieving system.

4. Pushing and Pulling

Uplifting leadership harnesses the power of the group to push and pull the team to complete their challenging journey together.

The secrets of achieving far above normal expectations are to be found in the fellowship of the team. Team members draw themselves and each other forward. If they get knocked down, they spring back up again and lift up those who have fallen around them. They also push each other to keep moving ahead. The team remains true to each other and to the common, inspiring purpose that binds them. We learn more about this kind of team spirit from Ireland's Gaelic Athletic Association (GAA) than we do from many professional sports organizations—where players on inflated wages with matching egos have no lasting commitment to each other or to a higher purpose beyond their own personal glory. And we will learn from an unusual multinational chemical company that operates as a commonwealth what needed to be done when teamwork degenerated into groupthink and the pull of the team began to undermine the push for success.

5. Measuring with Meaning

Uplifting leadership identifies indicators of direction and progress for navigating the route and for ascertaining how far an organization or system has come—and still has to go—in reaching its destination. Indications of early success build collective confidence and become a psychological investment for accepting greater struggles in the future. Every horizon that team members glimpse and then reach and every summit they surmount provides hope and optimism to continue the journey ahead. It both encourages and emboldens leaders and their teams to persist with their quest together. Uplifting leadership makes extensive use of data to manage and monitor progress, but also uses data intelligently in ways that fit the values of the organization—and that are *meaningful to* and *genuinely owned by* the people who work there. Our book will show how the "metric-obsessed" leaders at online footwear retailer Shoebuy.com used data intelligently—not just to respond swiftly to customer preferences, but also to add value to customer experience, empower employees to get involved in ongoing website experimentation and design, and complement the personal interactions between Shoebuy's management and customers.

6. Sustainable Success

Uplifting leadership takes off from a solid foundation and proceeds at a rate that does not consume everyone's effort and energy before they achieve the final objective. Leading people far above expectations is not merely initially successful; it must also be sustainable. Progress is rarely swift, and both leaders and team members must take care to avoid exhaustion as well as overreach. Although it can be exciting to *start* something new, uplifting leaders know that it is much harder to keep things going after they have started. Uplifting organizations and their leaders do not think about sustainability once the first flush of innovation has passed. They plan and prepare for it from the beginning. In this book, we read about start-ups like Shoebuy.com and Dogfish Head Craft Brewery that refused venture capital and turned down fancy equipment because they didn't want to get deep into debt or grow too quickly. We will see how turnarounds and changes that benefit many children in many schools in the poorest boroughs of London or whole countries like Finland do not happen overnight with sudden switches in leadership—but only after years of continuous and unrelenting commitment to stronger working relationships and greater success.

The Uplifting Journey

We derived these six factors of uplifting leadership that make up the journey to higher performance and purposes from our research. At times, our findings resonate with previous explanations of exceptional performance—especially research on inspirational and transformational leadership that highlights the "soft processes" that often underpin dramatically improved performance. These include having compelling visions of where to go, establishing a clear sense of direction of how to get there, and engaging the team in realizing that vision together.[18]

But other findings from our work sometimes depart from or even challenge these "soft skill" explanations in terms of the value they also attribute to old-fashioned hard work; the significance that is attached to hard data; and the continuing importance of bottom-line competition. Table I.1 distinguishes between the two extremes of "hard" and "soft" approaches to turnaround and uplift. We will show that it is not how we choose between these alternatives that defines exceptional success, but how we *combine them into one*. Finding common ground with those who most seek to oppose you, firing people with dignity, using your metrics to initiate personal phone calls with dissatisfied customers, and making sure that the spirit of innovation does not make guinea pigs of students or valued clients—these elements comprise the ironic essence of uplift.

In the organizations we examine, leaders of many kinds enhanced their peoples' performance by uplifting spirits, communities, and even themselves. They embarked on an epic journey together, and kept going by combining skills and qualities of a "soft" and "hard" nature that others might have regarded as mutually exclusive.

Table I.1 Approaches to Turnaround and Uplift

Soft	Hard
Dreaming	Persisting
Creating	Challenging
Collaborating	Competing
People-Centered	Data-Driven
Pulling	Pushing
Long-Term	Short-Term

Uplifting leadership pursues an improbable dream. People are prepared to fight for it with courage and tenacity. They chart unlikely courses that others have overlooked or even avoided. They use opposing forces to their advantage and employ data and indicators intelligently and in ways that involve the wider workforce or community. People measure their progress toward achieving their goals as a matter of collective responsibility more than top-down accountability. Uplifting leaders push and pull their teams to fulfill their dreams and to further each other's well-being as they move toward their destination. They make allies of their enemies and collaborate with their competitors. And they achieve all this not by the miracle cures and quick fixes that produce only temporary false recoveries, but by committing to sustainable growth that is relentless rather than reckless.

Let's see now just how uplifting leaders in all our organizations pulled all this together to achieve a lot with a little, create something from almost nothing, and turn failure into success.

Chapter One

Dreaming with Determination

With Dennis Shirley

All people dream, but not equally.
Those who dream by night in the dusty recesses of their mind,
Wake in the morning to find that it was vanity.
But the dreamers of the day are dangerous people,
For they dream their dreams with open eyes,
And make them come true.

—T. E. Lawrence

Dreaming and Believing

When Martin Luther King Jr. stood before the Reflecting Pool in Washington DC on a late August day in 1963, he did not declare that he had a *strategic plan*. He didn't list a set of key performance indicators or specify any targets for meeting them. Dr. King, as we know from his passionately delivered speech, had a dream—an improbable dream that his "four children will one day live in a nation where they will not be judged by the color of their skin but by the content of their character."[1] Within just two generations, that dream and all the actions it inspired helped give rise to the first African American president of the United States.

Without dreams, profound human and social change would scarcely be possible. Uplifting organizations and their leaders aspire to and articulate an improbable dream that is bolder than a plan or even a vision, and they inspire others to be part of it. Dreams like Martin Luther King's articulate the possibility of change and insist on its necessity.

Inspiring dreams is one of the very first factors that come into play when creating something from nothing or turning failure into success. Dreams describe an imaginable future to hope and strive toward, a vision that offers something far more desirable than the present state. Dreamers don't pressure people to change against their will; instead, they inspire people to change by eliciting, appealing to, and expressing their ideals, aspirations, and beliefs, so that they might believe in the possibility of unprecedented change.

Dreams are most powerful when they are held collectively by a community, rather than pursued for individual self-interest. The most inspiring dreams are therefore fundamentally connected to improving an entire organization, whole communities—even entire countries. These kinds of stimulating visions add meaning to people's lives and offer hope in the midst of despair. The following three elements of inspiration are especially integral to uplifting leadership and we will see them at work throughout this chapter and those that follow:

- A broad and inspiring dream **extends far beyond numerical targets**. It doesn't home in on being in the top five, or emphasize vague and lofty goals like being "world class." Instead, this kind of dream doesn't only promise to raise performance and increase output; it also strives to *change people's lives for the better*. It promises to bring them to a better place. This often occurs by inciting social uplift in terms of opportunity, equity, or advancement for those who have been marginalized or discriminated against. In two poor London boroughs that had been dogged by educational failure, the dream in Hackney was that parents would fight to get their children into its schools; in Tower Hamlets, it was that poverty would not be an acceptable excuse for failure.

- The dream's inclusive nature expresses **a sense of collective identity**. This means that the vision doesn't just belong to a few top leaders. It's also the property and prerogative of entire communities to which people form deep attachments, from the highest ranking executives to the lowest status assistants, from frontline workers to office staff in the back. The commonwealth at Scott Bader chemicals and resins creates an unbreakable bond of investment and involvement throughout the workforce that joins everyone together with a sense of social responsibility.

- The dream is made up of a **clearly articulated relationship between what has been and what will be**. It's not merely a description that harkens back to the past or looks toward the future, but that shows the connections and continuity between valued heritage and needed progress. This helps people to know where they are going by encouraging them to recall where they once started out. They are reminded what they are made of and where they came from. People in the small and economically depressed town of Burnley, in England, dared to dream that its soccer club could once again play in the top echelon of the English Premier League.

The power of inspiring dreams to raise collective performance and turn failure into success occurs in all kinds of places. One of the least likely junctures is where the rubber really does hit the road: in the auto-manufacturing industry. Yet this is just where we've found some of the most daring dreams of all. When Henry Ford established the Ford Motor Company, he declared that its purpose would be no less than "opening the highways to all mankind."[2]

On a crisp winter evening, the night before the 2009 US Presidential Inauguration, breaking news first reached the Italian City of Turin that would transform the city's and the world's understanding of its auto-manufacturing industry forever. The *Financial Times* was the first to report a possible partnership between Fiat Auto and American auto giant Chrysler.[3] Just months later, when Chrysler collapsed like a house of cards along with General Motors, the partnership became a reality. By the end of 2013, it was poised to turn into a full merger. On New Year's Day, 2014, Chrysler Motors and the United Autoworkers Union became "completely absorbed" by Fiat in a full merger when Fiat bought out the 41 percent share in Chrysler of the United Autoworkers Union Trust.[4]

Fabbrica Italiana Automobili Torino (FIAT) had come a long way from the brink of bankruptcy in 2004. Founded in 1899, Fiat had built a classic and honorable reputation throughout most of the twentieth century as one of the pioneers of the European car industry.[5] For a very long time, it was believed that what was good for Fiat Motors was also good for Italy as a nation. Fiat's Golden Age had taken place during the 1960s, when the tiny Fiat 500 was a market success and an iconic element in romantic European movies. Under Gianni Agnelli, grandson of the company's founder, Giovanni Agnelli, Fiat courted success through a chic sense of 1960s Italian style and quality.[6]

But signs of a slow decline at Fiat were already evident by the early 1980s. A robust yet overprotected domestic market in which Fiat sales peaked at 59 percent of market share in 1988, and a European market that still held up respectably at 15 percent, masked a host of underlying problems.[7] Whereas outsourcing represented only 50 percent of production in 1982, the figure had escalated to 65 percent a decade later—and similar patterns held for design work. The US market didn't just find Fiat's boxy vehicles unattractive; they were also unreliable. Warranty repair costs on the 1974 Fiat Strada wiped out all profits on its sales. By 1984, the company abandoned the US market altogether.[8]

A patrician style of management in this family-run company could no longer adapt to accelerated systems of production and to the increasingly globalized marketing of the modern auto-manufacturing industry. When Gianni Agnelli passed away in 2003, Fiat was in crisis. By 2004, the company had suffered seventeen straight quarters in the red.[9] A dizzying succession of four CEOs failed to produce a turnaround. Even the Mayor of Turin felt that Fiat was a "badly run company" that seemed headed for the wrecker's yard.[10]

In 2004, Sergio Marchionne was appointed as the first CEO ever to run Fiat Auto without the direct oversight of the Agnelli family. Even though he had no background in the industry, the company's problems were glaringly obvious to Marchionne when he took over. He described it as a "laughing stock," even a "cadaver."[11] Fiat had an overextended portfolio; its engineering focus had made it unappealing to stylish twenty-first-century consumers; and dealers had a take-it-or-leave-it attitude toward their customers.

Yet somehow, the company had returned to profitability as soon as 2006—and by 2008, before the global economic collapse, Fiat's bottom line was solidly in the black. In 2010, they were not merely surviving; they were overtaking and even *taking over* global competitors. The most dramatic of these was its audacious partnership with America's third-largest auto manufacturer, Chrysler, in the midst of the global economic collapse in 2009. As a leading Italian newspaper *La Repubblica*, expressed it: "Our little tin-plated sweetheart arrives in the land of the steel Cyclops to save them from their folly."[12]

To an enthralled business press, the oddball Canadian-Italian Marchionne was the company's savior—described as "strong," "visionary," "eccentric." There seemed to be an element of managerial machismo about the move to partner with

Chrysler, of course, but there was more to it than that. A big part of Marchionne's and Fiat's improbable dream was to bring small energy-efficient cars in great numbers to the US market. This move endeared Fiat to the Obama administration, and opened up the opportunity to form a partnership with Chrysler.[13] The move—which gave Chrysler access to small-car technology and smaller engines—would "help preserve American jobs" and "significantly accelerate Chrysler's efforts to produce fuel-efficient vehicles," Marchionne announced.[14] By the end of 2013, Fiat's share in this partnership had reached almost 60 percent.[15]

Fiat's commitment to making and marketing small, energy-efficient cars aligned with the global ambitions to combat climate change and to use energy resources prudently and profitably. Reducing waste—of fuel, materials, and energy—keeps costs down and is more environmentally responsible. To Sergio Marchionne, any waste is unethical.[16] Eventually, Fiat's goal is to reduce waste to zero.

Pursuing a moral or environmental purpose needn't make us sacrificial and sanctimonious—and that's something Fiat understands absolutely. People will not buy ugly cars, even if they are energy efficient. So just as it has through much of its history, Fiat associates itself with pleasure and style as well as profits and responsibility.

Before the move to partner and ultimately merge with Chrysler, Fiat had already launched the refashioned Cinquecento (500) and seen it become a great market success.[17] The new product linked cutting-edge innovation to a classic past. Fiat knows where it is going in part because it has reestablished pride *in where it has been*. Evoking people's youthful romanticism is one way to reengage them as drivers and designers of the future. Reconnecting customers with more youthful periods of hope, pride, and pleasure helps drive out any associations with failure in the recent past. The reinvention of classic brands provides a primal bridge from a better past to a brighter future.

Fiat's designers and advertisers are passionate about their products and the emotions they arouse. In a high-end European advertising campaign for Fiat's luxury Lancia brand, Hollywood actor and activist Richard Gere took a spiritual drive up to Tibet. Openly gay fashion icon Steffano Gabbana controversially kissed a descending black female angel. Here, purpose and pleasure, style and difference, moral dedication and passionate desire are strongly and often startlingly intertwined. The uplift is simultaneously emotional, social, and environmental. It connects Fiat's present to the best of its past while also linking its future to higher moral purposes of ecological responsibility and human rights. It uses inspiration to forge an aesthetic and ethical identity. Succeeding for its own sake is not Fiat's goal. Embedding success within an emotionally inspirational and socially responsible sense of the better life that success can bring is more emblematic of the company's future aspirations and original identity.

Fiat is not the first or the only organization to uplift performance by using inspirational goals, images, myths, and narratives that remind people of the best versions of who they are, what they once were, and who they truly want to be. Other organizations have demonstrated this ability to forge powerful and positive connections between the future and the past, between inspiration and identity. We see another such example in the world of sports.

When the US women's soccer team lost its top position in the world rankings, the team members' dream was not to retain the Number 1 slot. Rather, they sought to "raise the level of sport for women everywhere" and "be part of the worldwide social revolution which sees women fulfilling a different role in society."[18] They did so by donating more voluntary time to local community events and projects where they were playing than their male counterparts in Major League Soccer were doing. Women's sport has gained more and more attention annually since the US women's soccer team set these goals in 1991. And along the way, the team also won the World Cup in 1999.

When Gary Erikson invented the popular energy snack Clif Bar, which he named after his adventuresome dad, his goal was to combine his love of adventure with the passion he developed for cooking in his mother's kitchen. Erikson wanted to produce a tasty, nutritious alternative to the bland, highly processed power bars available in 1990. Clif Bar's brand vision became simply "sustaining people in motion."[19] Its annual reports don't only or even mainly issue financial data to shareholders. Instead, they set out other indicators of the company's contribution to sustainable development and healthy eating—including growth in use of organic ingredients, donations to valued nonprofits, and limiting the company's ecological footprint. Commenting on a challenging national recall of tainted peanut products, the company's 2009 report affirmed that Clif Bar had for fifteen years "been able to make financial decisions based on a long-term vision of a healthy business rather than short-term requirements that limit costs and maximize short-term profits," and that its disciplined philosophy of "living within its means" had enabled it to "weather the storm."[20] As Erickson points out in his book *Raising the Bar*, "These ideals inspire and motivate our work."[21]

What we learn from organizations as dissimilar as Fiat, Clif Bar, and US Women's Soccer is the power of reaching for something greater than fame or success for their own sake—whether it is ecological responsibility, health and fitness, or women's opportunities and success. In his book *The Good Struggle*, Joseph Badaracco describes this as "reaching the heights"—not just of performance numbers, but also of social purpose and emotional excitement.[22] Reaching the heights is the first thing to do when you are after uplift. Most people have heard the famous tale of President Kennedy asking a cleaner at NASA what his job was. The cleaner replied, "To put a man on the moon." Both the president and the NASA employee grasped this concept: the first thing to do is to articulate the improbable dream. The more important thing is that everybody, not just you, comes to believe it.

Uplifting leadership is not primarily about a number or a ranking that utilizes envy as its overriding emotion. It is found in what a community aspires to become and in how this serves a greater good. Instead of having no dreams, idle dreams, or hollow dreams, filled only with the indicators of self-seeking success, uplifting leadership is about an inspiring and inclusive dream that draws people upwards by addressing their desire for self-actualization, their needs for service to the community, and their wish to be part of something bigger than themselves. It articulates a dream that defines a desirable destination for people, and does so in ways that are consistent with the best of what they once were or what they have always been.

Dreaming and Daring

The kind of inspiration that uplifts people, organizations, and communities is more than an idle wish or a fancy speech; it must also instigate powerful, new, and deliberate actions. It is evident in what people *do* as well as what they say, and requires courage, daring, and determination to bring it to fruition.

People don't always greet dreams and their dreamers with instant adulation. More often than not, bold visions provoke incomprehension, opposition, ridicule, and doubt. When Alexander Graham Bell took his patent to the Telegraph Company, which later became known as Western Union, the response was that this "ungainly and impractical device" was not as good as sending a messenger to the telegraph office.[23] Uplifting leaders and their first followers are not defeated by these doubts; rather, they are emboldened by them. They enjoy having others underestimate them because doubt and derision just fuel their determination to succeed.

Individuals who have led others through profound change do not do so without fear of failure, danger, or what the future might hold in store. Every leader experiences a moment of self-doubt where he or she faces the real prospect of defeat. What defines uplifting leadership is how these individuals deal with their own and their followers' fear—and do so in a way that creates uplift.

There will always be questions that test the scruples of even the most effective leaders: "Have I promised too much?" "Will I let people down?" "Do I have the stamina to see this through?" "Am I exploiting people for my own ambition?" But such leaders do not freeze in the headlights or take flight at times of self-reflection and even self-doubt. Instead, the improbable dream and formidable challenge of surmounting failure, escaping closure, or avoiding bankruptcy instill a sense of determination to overcome barriers to change and see the process through to victory.

Facing down opponents to a dream requires that leaders act with personal courage, strength, and fortitude. Such a response calls on everyone to find something within themselves they may never have realized they had. This process calls upon people who are prepared to fight and to elevate entire communities.

Dean Vogel, Eric Heins, and Mary Rose Ortega are leaders who embody such qualities. They lead an organization that has been helping hundreds of the lowest performing schools in California—those that are in the bottom 20 percent of student achievement—to turn around. The kind of organization that is doing this work may well surprise you, and we shall reveal its identity shortly; but first let's learn a little more about these three leaders. All of them are dedicated, dyed-in-the-wool teachers. Vogel, the organization's president, was an elementary school teacher and an award-winning school counselor for thirty-nine years. Ortega, a member of its board of directors, taught in challenging inner-city Los Angeles elementary schools for almost as long. She decided to become a teacher as a young student because she was prevented from using her Spanish language skills to translate for a new immigrant student from Mexico. Eric Heins, the youngest of the three, is a former music teacher who "got tired of watching the arts being eliminated" when schools devoted more and more time to driving up test score results by teaching to the test. Heins just wanted to "get back to good teaching" by engaging children with their learning.

There's no denying that this organization had its work cut out for it. In a half-century's time, California went from being one of the most admired educational systems—with an average spending per pupil above the national average and graduation rates climbing annually—to a wasteland of educational underachievement. Funding fell below the national average in 2000; by 2003, California's students performed worse on the National Assessment of Educational Progress than all other US states except Louisiana and Mississippi.[24]

Yet even in the face of all this, Vogel, Heins, and Ortega's organization—the California Teachers' Association (CTA), the largest state teachers' union in the United States—is showing encouraging results.[25] A report by the California Department of Education found that "an analysis of the Academic Performance Index (API) of participating schools indicates that their average performance exceeded the average performance of schools statewide, as well as an appropriate comparison group of schools in the early years of the program."[26] In other words, the schools participating in this program progressed at a faster rate than those that were not in the program. An independent research evaluation also found that "on average, schools are making greater gains with African American and Hispanic students, English Language Learners, and socioeconomically disadvantaged students than similar schools."[27]

The work the CTA has done and the admirable results it has achieved do not seem to fit with the less-than-flattering portrayal of teachers' unions in the media. Indeed, they have been given quite a thrashing in recent years. The multi-million-dollar movie *Waiting for Superman* shows shocking instances of teachers' unions failing to deal with incompetent members at great cost to the system. In *Special Interest: Teachers' Unions and American Public Schools*, Stanford University political scientist Terry Moe attacks teachers' unions for defending their own special interests at the expense of the public interest.[28] And *Wall Street Journal* editorial writer Peter Brimelow provocatively titled his own book on teacher unions *The Worm in the Apple: How Teacher Unions Are Destroying American Education.*[29]

So when the California Teachers' Association set out to help large numbers of Californian schools to turn around, it had a real fight on its hands. Vogel, Heins, and Ortega knew they'd have to fight for the educational rights and opportunities of the state's most disadvantaged students. They were prepared to dispel public and political stereotypes about the threat of teacher unions and the damage they supposedly cause. And they had to lead a fight within the union itself to embark upon a new vision of where the organization—and the whole teacher union movement—should be going. But before facing all these obstacles, the CTA had one of the biggest fights of its life—with the state's governor, Arnold Schwarzenegger.

Governor Schwarzenegger is as formidable an opponent in real life as he is in the movies. Indeed, California's Governator had a personal life narrative and a knockabout style that led voters to return him to office in a landslide election in 2006. However, CTA leaders were not part of the popular support for the governor. They were in fact outraged when Schwarzenegger removed billions of dollars from the education budget to address shortfalls across the system. So in August 2005, the union sued Schwarzenegger for violating the rulings of previous court cases that required the state to allocate a defined percentage of its revenues to education, especially for low-income students of color. In a ruling in the May 2006 case of *CTA v. Governor Schwarzenegger*, the California Supreme Court sided with the teachers' union.[30] The governor was ordered to restore $2.3 billion to the education budget on terms to be negotiated with the CTA. The CTA had won its first fight and perhaps its biggest one. But in other ways, the battle had barely begun.

CTA's next struggle was internal, as it attempted to answer the question: what would it do with its gold-plated opportunity? It did not disburse the $2.3 billion to its members in salary and benefits or simply spread the money across the schools on a per capita basis. This would have ignored the system's vast funding inequities between affluent and impoverished school districts. Instead, the union designed and implemented a change model that ran against the grain of other models that school systems throughout America were adopting.

Plenty of other US educational reforms had taken place in school systems that had registered persistently poor results. These districts and state departments frequently trumpeted their uncompromising decisions to fire principals, remove teachers, close down schools, and parachute in no-nonsense turnaround teams—efforts that had little lasting or widespread success, and that only provided temporary recoveries.[31] Others came at the expense of taking the best teachers or students from neighboring schools. The CTA took a different approach and decided to work *with*—not against—the teaching profession. It turned teachers into change leaders in every turnaround school, right across the state.

The CTA began by allocating resources to a **teacher leader** in each school. As Mary Rose Ortega explained, "It's the *teachers* who know what the kids need . . . [who] should be [providing] input into what is being done at their schools with these kids." The goal was not for teachers to be left autonomous and alone; rather, it was to bring professionals together to take *collective responsibility* for student achievement and school improvement. They took steps toward this outcome by visiting each other's classes to give constructively critical feedback on how to improve their teaching, and by looking at student achievement data together to pinpoint where they could make interventions. As one educator remarked during an in-depth independent evaluation of thirty-four of the schools, "We have a lot of collaboration time now; and it's part of our goal to look at data to increase student achievement. We have data teams on Wednesdays to assess test scores and come up with strategies for improvement."[32] Teacher collaboration wasn't infrequent or sporadic; it occurred at least weekly. Professional development was related to precise needs that these collaborative groups identified rather than appealing to individual teacher preferences or exposing educators to the thinking of the latest gurus.

Eric Heins drove us to one of the CTA's project schools, just over an hour out of San Francisco, to see their project in action. The school had recently pulled itself out of what is called "program improvement"—that is, it had not made what the state and federal government regarded as "Adequate Yearly Progress" for two years in a row. Teachers who criticized the school's previous long-standing principal had been punished. They were assigned classes in new grade levels each year, which meant extra preparation, constant disruption, and a much harder time hitting their test score targets.

Many school reformers had a habit of regarding experienced teachers like these as old, expensive, and in the way. But the new principal "was willing to learn," as one of the veteran teachers recalled. "We started exchanging articles and books," and when he really started "asking a million questions," he saw a group of highly experienced, knowledgeable, and dedicated educators who had become disheartened under the previous principal's top-down, divide-and-rule turnaround strategies. The new principal realized that, as a group, his teachers knew more about highly effective teaching practices than he did. Several had been involved in a nationally regarded project where schools worked together to improve literacy achievement. Others had given up their own time to connect with outstanding professionals across the country to improve students' writing skills. Like all good leaders, this principal realized that his job was not to be smarter than his teachers at their jobs, but to get them to collaborate more effectively and capitalize on their skills collectively.

Teacher leaders in the school used the CTA money to employ additional teacher support. This allowed them to meet with colleagues during the day to look at their students' achievement data together. Teachers also visited other schools in the region that seemed to be realizing improved results with similar kinds of students. They learned from their colleagues and from other schools, and they improved by moving their professional capital around the system more effectively.

Despite the fact that the school had been losing its higher-performing students and families to competing charter schools and a more affluent neighborhood school, indicators of school achievement "went off the charts" as a result of all these efforts. Results also rose steadily across the network, especially among the most disadvantaged groups of students from minorities or from families in poverty who were uplifted by the union's efforts.

Educators were uplifted too. Many of the state's most experienced teachers—who had felt slightly beaten down by reform methods that demanded compliance instead of commitment—were able to put their rich professional capital into use and spread it around. And when teachers turned into uplifting leaders along with their principals, this uplifted the union as well.

The CTA's shift in focus to improving student achievement in almost four hundred schools resonated with its members' core values. Concentrating on children and their learning "is the norm [for us]," one teacher said. "It's [our] intrinsic [goal]." Many young teachers became inspired and uplifted by a union that was now more professionally oriented and explicitly morally centered—something that now felt like it could be the right place for them.

You and your organization won't be able to achieve very much for very long unless your success is motivated by an inspiring dream. And you will not achieve your dreams or maintain the momentum to do so unless you fight for them tooth and nail. The California Teachers Association took on and won a monumental legal fight against Governor Arnold Schwarzenegger because its leaders felt morally called to protect and uplift the state's most underserved students. They knew that this also meant they would have to fight for a more noble identity and a higher professional self within their own community by reinventing what teacher unions were professionally and what they stood for publicly.

Leadership that creates something from nothing or turns failure into success is not for the faint-hearted. It requires not only visions and dreams, but also the hard work and struggle to make them come true. In *Leadership and the Art of Struggle*, author Steven Snyder describes how flawed individuals perform remarkable leadership in the face of adversity because they're able to stay grounded in their lives and to understand where their own struggles come from. They take new pathways that others have not explored, and persist and adapt even in the face of personal hardship.[33] Snyder cites many legendary examples, such as Abraham Lincoln, Bill Gates, and Steve Jobs. But some of the best examples of individuals who have had to face some very daunting leadership struggles involve women.

Josephine Cochrane wasn't looking for fame or fortune when she invented the self-operating mechanical dishwasher in 1886. She simply felt that if women could be spared the drudgery of working in their kitchens, she would have to create the solution herself. However, after receiving her first patent, Cochrane encountered reluctance to adopt the idea for the domestic market—not least because many men feared that with access to mechanical contraptions to perform their domestic labor, women might then be left with dangerously idle time on their hands. So Cochrane took her invention into another market instead: to large institutions such as great hotels, which adopted her invention in numbers after a successful showing at the Chicago World's Fair in 1893. In an interview some years later, Cochrane recalled what things were like before the Fair, when she was trying to get her first hotel sales: "You cannot imagine what it was like in those days for a woman to cross a hotel lobby alone. I had never been anywhere without my husband or father—the lobby seemed a mile wide. I thought I should faint at every step, but I didn't—and I got an $800 order as my reward."[34]

What are you prepared to fight for? What would you stake your reputation and career on? These questions will help you uncover the fight and fortitude that characterizes uplifting leadership to take the difficult but necessary path. It points you away from what's merely easy and compels you to put in the hard yards if that is what it will take to achieve your moral purpose and inspiring dream.

Dreaming and Doing

Of course, dreams matter little unless you *do* something about them. Inspiration changes nothing unless it is translated into action. However admirable or bold your dreams might be about transforming the driving habits of a nation, they will come to nothing if your auto-manufacturing company goes out of business. Despite the disarming informality of his open-neck shirt appearance, Sergio Marchionne knew that Fiat would not survive unless it cut the design-to-production process from four years to an unprecedented period of eighteen and then fifteen months.[35] So he worked at an astounding pace to turn Fiat's inspiring dream into achievable and detailed action.[36]

There comes a point when persistence, perseverance, and relentless hard work are essential to almost all acts of uplifting leadership, especially in turnaround situations. "When you're going through Hell," Winston Churchill once advised, "keep going!"[37] Aside from inspiration, organizations in pursuit of an improbable dream also need a lot of perspiration and, sometimes, even a bit of desperation to keep them going.

At times, this intense experience of endurance can define the difference between extinction and survival, between keeping one foot out of the grave even though the other may have slipped into it. It's inspiring to be uplifting when things are buoyant. It's *essential* to be uplifting when they are not. When Lehman Brothers collapsed in September 2008 it set off a global financial crisis that shook the world. Let's take a peek at how one of America's largest businesses, worth around $54 billion, dealt with this crisis, lifted itself through the global recession, and came out stronger than before.[38]

The DuPont HQ in Wilmington, Delaware, is the hub of a 212-year-old, *market-driven science* company with spokes into ninety countries around the globe and employs a workforce of sixty-five thousand. Since it began in 1802, DuPont has pioneered the frontiers of science and invented synthetic materials such as Teflon, Lycra, Kevlar, and Dacron. It manufactured materials used in hundreds of familiar household products that uphold their promises to be nonstick, wrinkle-free, lightweight, or flexible.[39]

In an interview for Ernst and Young, DuPont CEO Ellen Kullman recalls the severity of the financial crisis. "Demand collapsed in every country, in every business outside of agriculture, in a three-month period of time, and it was totally unprecedented. We've seen what we thought were some bad recessions, but none of us had ever seen anything like that before."[40] Loyal customers cancelled orders; sales volumes halved in some parts of the company; and employees were worried about their future. DuPont needed to respond quickly. Change was mandatory; growth was optional.

DuPont had a long and successful history of growth from its commitment to innovation through science that Kullman valued as part of its long-standing identity. She recognized that the way to grow during the global recession was through *continued and expanding scientific innovation*—bringing new products to new markets. Her dream was to change DuPont from a chemical company to a *market-driven science* company that would find scientific solutions to feed the world's growing population, create more energy sources and protect people from environmental disasters.[41] DuPont turned doomsday scenarios of famine, energy shortages, and disasters into opportunities for growth.

Kullman achieved this first by making difficult but essential cuts—for instance, reducing capital spending to zero. The company coached sales executives to re-engage with former customers by visiting them personally. They recast existing products for new markets, such as a chemical designed for India's railways to China.[42]

Second, they had to rethink their business model and develop service-based ways of engaging with customers—including one with Denso Corp to develop a high-performance plastic from renewable plants for the global auto industry. They won new business as a result. Kullman is clear about this new approach to invention: "we strongly believe that the power of innovation resides in collaboration with our partners."[43] In Mexico, as part of what they call their *Global Collaboratory*, DuPont partnered with a company called Repshel to develop low-cost but strong building materials from polymers and titanium dioxide products. Repshel then collaborated with the government to build affordable and safe family homes in Campeche, Mexico. This kind of collaboration transforms people's lives.[44]

DuPont understands that no single organization alone will solve the complex issues around food, energy supply, and personal safety that face the world's ever-growing population. But by collaborating closely with customers, governments, and other providers, DuPont believes that science can create innovative solutions that will eradicate poverty, provide sustainable energy, and protect individuals and the environment. DuPont, which began by making explosives for the US government, has consciously shifted its ethical stance from once being labeled as one of the world's biggest polluters to being an award winner in environmental and social responsibility.[45]

Kullman found it easier to get people to think differently when their future was so uncertain. But she also understood how to manage the pace of change in a way that would keep her own organization sustainable, "If you try to change everybody at once, you're changing nobody," she said, "so you really have to start in one area, or a couple of areas, and show success."[46]

The third element of this approach was that—at a time when everyone was adopting the reasonable response of keeping their heads down until the worst was over—Kullman insisted on open, hopeful, and constant communication. She made it a point to maintain consistency of message and direction about how to respond to the crisis and not just survive, but be more successful. Maintaining the mission was essential, and communication was vital when DuPont underwent two restructurings in five months that cut 4,500 jobs (8 percent of the workforce) and imposed furloughs without pay. Kullman went on from there. "We set to further streamline and simplify the company, and we took out a layer of leadership and got really clear on what success looks like coming out of the recession."[47]

Under Kullman's leadership, DuPont is now in a better position with higher growth and higher value than when she took over. Getting the company to respond to a change of direction at a time of such uncertainty required powerful uplifting leadership. Revenue grew throughout the recession and the stock market value rose by 119 percent from 2009 to 2014.[48]

This is how you enact uplifting leadership. You struggle together to survive, but you also strive to succeed—and you do both these things at once. You remind yourself of your origins and recast your mission in relation to it. You keep on innovating, even in a recession, but you do so in collaboration with your partners and respond to their local needs. You make the *market drive your business*, rather than the other way round. And you learn your way forward all the time. Kullman reminds us that DuPont is always learning: "We've seen pretty much everything that two centuries of a turbulent world history can throw at a company. We're still here because we *learned* to be resilient. We *learned* how to use science to innovate, and we *learned* how to transform ourselves in an ever-changing world."[49]

If you fail to survive in the corporate world, you go out of business. And if you fail to survive in sports—you also go out of business! Yet one of the best ways to survive is to strive to succeed, far beyond everyone's expectation—even when everything seems against you.

In September of 2006, Dave Edmundson—chief executive of a tiny English football (soccer) club—led his staff retreat to redefine the club's purpose: achieving promotion to the English Premier League of Soccer, the biggest and wealthiest global sporting brand in the world. The audacious goal was "to become a premier club that will achieve Premier League status."[50]

The title of the presentation for Burnley Football Club's retreat seemed like outrageous overreach. Burnley had just spent several seasons sitting in the middle reaches of the second-tier Championship Division—the one below the Premier League. But even that had been an over-achievement. Its wage bills and ticket sales ranked 20th out of twenty-four in the championship. The small Northern mill town is among the 7 percent of the most deprived communities in England.[51] Its entire population of around eighty thousand would not even fill the stadium for Manchester United. Club Chairman Barry Kilby, constantly stressed how the club "punches above its weight" and Alastair Campbell—one-time "spin doctor" for Prime Minister Tony Blair and also a lifetime Burnley fan—believed that "promotion to the Premier League in some ways defied footballing gravity."[52]

Less than three years later, in May 2009, we sat with more than twenty thousand Burnley fans at London's new Wembley Stadium to watch the team win the championship playoff final and fulfill its improbable dream of moving into the Premier League. Emblazoned on the back of the fans' shirts was the club's slogan "Dare to Dream."

How did Burnley achieve so much with so little? How did the club rise from mediocrity into the highest echelons of sporting success? How did it become the smallest town ever to join the English Premier League, with less assets, investment, and support than all its Premier League counterparts?

In fairness, the club didn't completely start with nothing or come from nowhere. It had a fine and proud tradition as one of the twelve founding members of the English Football League in 1888. In the early 1960s, Burnley was also champion of the old First Division (the equivalent of today's Premier League).

Tradition and nostalgia count for something, but they are not enough to feed continuing success. Over the next twenty-five years, Burnley sank to rock bottom among ninety-two clubs in the English Football League. Before the very final game of the season in 1987, their place as the last club positioned them for elimination from the Football League altogether. Burnley was on the edge of extinction.

In the boardroom of Burnley Football Club today, a framed player's shirt hangs prominently on the oak-paneled wall. It does not belong to the club's highest goal scorer or its biggest playing legend. It is the shirt of an unknown, lower-league, bit-part player named Ian Britton whose career would have passed without incident had it not been for a single act he performed that inscribed him in club history forever. Although he was the smallest man on the field and one of the shortest in the game, Britton leapt above all his opponents and scored the winning goal with his head in the crucial final match of the 1987 season. In one split second, Britton lifted Burnley up from the bottom position and kept them in the Football League.

Sometimes, organizations behave like addicts: they have to hit rock bottom before they are willing to change. Almost losing everything is the kind of wake-up call that presents a crucial choice: to give in and go under or to stand up and fight. It is the moment of desperation that sometimes has to precede a period of inspiration. Burnley's near-death experience was the start of a long recovery: a crisis that galvanized a collective determination to change.

Today, Britton's shirt represents a perverse kind of inspiration. It reminded Chairman Barry Kilby and others of where they came from, of how neglect and excessive indebtedness could imperil the town and the team, and of the need to fight for one's destiny not just during a crisis but also as a relentless quest. The shirt is a reminder that at Burnley, the fight for survival is endless, and that preparedness to keep on fighting every minute of every day can define the dividing line between failure and success. It is not the kind of fight that can be captured only in moments of dramatic conflict. It is the fight that gets people out of bed every day even though they may have lost their partners or their jobs. It is the fight that spurs people on to try again and try harder after every failure or defeat. It is the fight to give everything in time, money, or energy, to a cause that is overwhelmingly important to them. It is the kind of fight that calls not only for daredevil brinksmanship, but also for grim determination, and even drudgery.

Burnley's dream and the everyday hard graft of turning it into reality are rooted in the club's inspirational identity. Burnley's first dream was not just to ascend into the English Premier League, but also to use this to achieve an even bigger dream that was about a "club for its people" that would be the "beating heart of its community, on and off the pitch." Everyone was urged to "pull on the shirt" for Burnley, even and especially whenever the fates seemed against them.

It took more than a quarter century for Burnley to fall and almost the same time for it to rise again. A succession of shrewdly chosen coaches (known in England as "managers"), along with prudent investment from local business entrepreneur and former youth team player Barry Kilby, who joined Burnley as its new chairman in 1998, helped the club to find its feet again, to the point where it was enjoying stable if not stellar success in the championship.

Then, in the middle of 2002, a sudden withdrawal of income from television rights plunged Burnley into an unexpected battle for economic survival. The club instantly lost £6 million in cash flow that it had been counting on over two years. At one point, it was just half an hour from declaring bankruptcy. Chairman Barry Kilby recalled how Burnley found itself in a "scramble for our lives," "scrapping away," "dealing with losses wherever we could."[53] The playing squad was reduced by almost a third, the wage bill was almost halved, external debts were paid off, others were restructured on an interest-only basis, and two key players were sold. All of this helped, but it still wasn't enough.

In the midst of the crisis, Burnley appointed former change consultant Dave Edmundson as its new chief executive. Edmundson's immediate rescue strategy was up-by-the-bootstraps stuff. He felt that the club needed to sell more "walk-on" or "buy-on-the-day" tickets on the day games were played to compensate for a drop in advanced ticket sales, so he led a highly publicized *Walk up for Burnley* campaign by walking ten miles to work himself. He also persuaded 150 people to donate £1,000 each, which, he reckoned, "really made a huge difference."

Burnley knew it could draw on its employees' and supporters' loyalty and attachment to the team. "I think the club got to that low point," Edmundson reflected, "and then it was a case of 'OK boys, it's time to roll our sleeves up and do what do we need to do to get out of it.'" Sometimes this backs-to-the-wall struggle seemed desperate—sponsored bike rides, cash collections in plastic buckets, or telemarketing drives to improve ticket sales. One eight-year-old girl sent the manager a small bag of silver coins—her own Christmas present—as her contribution to the cause. "I carry that letter round with me to this day and read it in public," Edmundson tells.

All the effort and determination paid off. The club's connections to its struggling local community became an asset rather than a liability. Incoming Operational Director Brendan Flood knew that the team could count on the investments he promised because "they knew I was a big fan." Edmundson's successor, Paul Fletcher, was set on "putting something back" into the club that developed him as a player. In the words of one of the members of the senior administrative team who actually doubled up on two jobs, they all "believe in the cause," "go the extra mile" and give "that little bit extra."

Once Burnley had survived the crisis and received the additional input of modest outside investment, they were able to dream really big in future years—and to turn that dream into reality. Even the team's new inspirational and enthusiastic coach, Owen Coyle, was selected because he also possessed the qualities of grit and determination that ran throughout the club as a whole. He was seen as a battler, a "tryer," who knew how to fight his way up from poverty and out of trouble.[54] Coyle came from a big Catholic family in the notorious Gorbals, the slums of Glasgow. He was a lifelong teetotaler who worked hard, stayed focused, and didn't get distracted. In other words, he was the ideal person to continue the tradition of uplifting leadership for the team.

"I started out as a part-time player at the bottom," Coyle recalled. "So I think having worked as hard as I did, I knew I could do well." Coyle also knew that like him, most players came up from nothing. Amid all the glamour and distractions, he constantly reminded them where they came from. He wasn't interested in "players who are going to be chasing finance." He wanted the ones "who are hungry," and proud to play for "that Burnley shirt on their back." The best players, in his view, were those that supporters could be proud of and say, "He might not have had the best game today, but by God he's a tryer."

Coyle didn't see fighting and trying as dour acts of survival, but rather as dynamic drivers of success. He and his coaching team were enthusiastic and uplifting leaders. They believed in themselves, the team, and the purpose they were seeking to achieve together. Players paid tribute to how "enthusiastic" Coyle was;

they told of how "he believes in us so much as individuals and as a team." The club became "a happy place to come to, and that vibrancy and buoyancy is evident in our play."[55]

With this combination of inspiration and determination, the team clinched a place in the English Premiership. And although the circling wolves of competitive commercial soccer came to snatch Coyle and all of his managerial team away in mid-season, sending the club back to the championship again at season's end, it returned with a $100 million bounty that resulted from having secured premiership status. Its culture of shrewd investment and hard work—along with the inspired appointment of another coach on October 30, 2012—has only perpetuated Burnley's success. New coach Sean Dyche also knows how to combine uplifting inspiration with dogged determination by believing in his small squad of bargain-priced players, while also being very direct and honest with them. One of the club's most mercurial players, known for having battles with his fitness and his attitude in the past, described how he was "lower than a snake's belly" until Dyche came in. Dyche used his "man management" skills to be "straight" with the player and gave him another chance to realize his considerable creative potential on the field.[56] As we go to press in 2014, the club has secured automatic promotion to the English Premier League once more, far beyond everyone's expectations.

Conclusion

If dreams are about envisaging reaching a desired destination, however improbable or remote, then they are also about reaffirming an organization's or community's identity. They recapture and redefine the best of what the organization or community has been in the past as a platform for creating a better future. Groups that cannot do this may be unable to imagine what they might become because they have no grasp of who they have been or already are.

As exemplified by Fiat, Burnley, and the California Teachers' Association, uplifting leadership is therefore contingent upon much more than having a goal or a set of aspirations. The difference between high and exceptional performance comes down to the extent to which **members subscribe to and genuinely believe in the organization's values, vision, and core principles.** Working within exceptional companies, teams, and groups is not simply a job, but a life choice. It calls for bold imagination yet also draws on grim determination—the willingness to persist, despite all obstacles, in pursuit of a commonly held and deeply cherished dream.

We will see later how the citizens of Finland built one of the world's highest performing school systems and strongest economies from the wreckage of high unemployment in 1992. They have a word that sums up the uplifting qualities of fight and fortitude: *sisu*. This term, a self-acknowledged national characteristic, means to persevere despite all obstacles. A common saying among Finns after a characteristically cold winter or after any significant shared struggle is "It was long and it was hard but we did it."

Do you and your organization have *sisu*? Can you persevere and prevail? For, in the end, *sisu* is the determined long game of what makes uplifting dreams come true. And the place you might least expect but be most in need of it, is in the midst of upbeat waves of innovation and creativity when brainstorming is rampant and ideas are in full flow. As we will see in the next chapter, without the discipline and determination of *sisu*, most attempts at creativity will come to nothing at all.

Chapter Two

Creativity and Counter-Flow

With Alex Gurn, Corrie Stone Johnson, Pak Tee Ng

Creativity comes from a conflict of ideas.

—*Donatella Versace*

Opposite Approach

Once you know where you are going and have people who are prepared to fight with you to get there, which way should you go? Should you follow the well-worn paths of those before you, taking trails that your competitors have already blazed? Or should you adopt a different or even opposing approach—what Robert Frost called in one of his most famous poems "The Road Not Taken"?[1]

In his book *How the Weak Win Wars*, Boston University Professor Ivan Arreguin-Toft examines what happens when weak armies prevail over opponents with far superior resources.[2] Strong armies, he says, win wars by copying their rivals' strategies and overpowering the opposition. But weak armies win wars by adopting *unconventional* strategies that their opponents do not expect. America took one of its first great strides toward independence when its colonists refused to stand up and fight in the open with proper uniforms against their red-coated British opponents, but wore everyday clothes and hid behind trees as their imperial enemy stumbled its way to ignominious defeat.

We saw in the Introduction how in the field of physics the original aerodynamic concept of lift or uplift is equally counterintuitive. How can the world's largest passenger airliners possibly take off, fully loaded, with weights of more than half a million pounds each? They do this by harnessing the basic force that makes many kinds of flight, including human flight, possible. In simple terms, this involves getting air to move over the wings faster than the air below them. When that happens, the air pressure underneath exceeds that above and the wings lift up. If the air moves fast enough, the pressure difference is big enough to carry the loaded plane with them. So, instead of running with the wind, it helps to take off *against* it, with the right speed and the wings tilted at the correct angle. The flow of air becomes the secret of the uplift that raises metal monsters far into the sky.

Organizations that are prepared to run against the mainstream and "into the wind" can create uplift not by going *with* the flow, but rather by moving against or around it. Uplifting leadership is courageous, creative, and fundamentally counterintuitive. It welcomes argument and disagreement. Uplifting leaders find resistance to be a source of energy and learning, and they welcome the opportunity to harness its capacities.

Uplifting leaders know they have to breathe out when they are coming up for air. They accelerate through the corner and steer into the skid. In times of crisis, scarcity, or threat, they expand when others contract, make the first move instead of following the rest, and combine with competitors instead of scrambling for shrinking resources against them. They do the exact opposite of what others expect of them in a very deliberate way. When uplifting leaders take on counterintuitive challenges of this sort, they enter a state that Sir Ken Robinson describes as being in their "element." They pursue their quest with a passion and intensity that is utterly absorbing for them. The Element, Robinson argues, "is the meeting point between natural aptitude and personal passion" where people "connect with something fundamental to their sense of identity, purpose and well-being."[3] Uplifting leaders who are successful at taking creative and counterintuitive paths for a greater good are in their element as leaders, and they are equally successful in enabling their followers to find their element too.

Against the Grain

It takes guts and gall for a business to move in the direction that's the opposite of where everyone else is headed. Yet this is the essence of innovation and entrepreneurship—to see an opportunity that your competitors have missed and to make a move that nobody else expects. Some organizations just see the crescent, while others see the whole of the moon. The point of counterintuitive thinking is not to be contrarian for its own sake. Rather, it is to see something important that others have missed, and to seize the moment in exploring and exploiting it.

Fiat decided to convert much of the US public to using small, fuel-efficient cars at a time when American obsessions with size and power made it likely that the risk was actually reckless. At the turn of the century, Finnish telecommunications giant Nokia was a world leader in mobile phone technology and sales when it rejected touch-screen technologies that its innovators were developing—because, in the recollection of Frank Nuovo, Nokia's mobile phone designer, "all of our user testing pointed to the fact that no-one wanted touch phones." Then "Apple pounced" with its "App."[4] Its iPhone became far more than a tool for communication and generated more revenue from selling apps than from the phones themselves. Similarly, the decision of Starbucks to demarcate the coffee market at a time when the main options were black or with cream, instant or brewed, went against the grain of existing customer choice in coffee purchasing and created vast new areas of demand.[5]

Although our study didn't look at coffee retailers directly, we did examine counterintuitive thinking in the production of another popular beverage: beer. Beer brewing is mainly a mass-production industry in which just two companies—MillerCoors and Anheuser-Busch InBev—occupy almost 80 percent of the US market share.[6] In corporate terms, beer is a stronghold of these two big battalions. In the mid-1990s, a man named Sam Calagione decided to take them on.

Sam was waiting tables at an Upper West Side restaurant in New York City to support himself while he was studying writing when he learned about alternative craft beers and became a fan. At the back of his small apartment, he brewed up concoctions for a few friends. They liked what they tasted. Sam went on to establish a combined restaurant and brewery, known as a brew-pub, in Milton, Delaware. He gave his beer the memorably quirky name of Dogfish Head, after a place where he used to vacation as a child.

Though these were small beginnings, Sam dreamed that he would eventually be responsible for a new, nationally known brand that would disrupt the definition of beer. Today, Dogfish Head Craft Brewery is one of the most successful independent breweries in the United States. In 2008, it ranked 22nd among top craft brewing companies by sales volume.[7] In the past decade it has averaged 40 percent yearly revenue growth. This compares with a mean growth rate of just 2.1 percent in the American beer industry as a whole.[8]

However, what's more telling than mere growth is the cult status that Dogfish Head has achieved. The beer company and its CEO, Sam Calagione, have been featured in *The New Yorker*, on the *Discovery Channel*, in a full-length film entitled *Beer Wars*, and in several highly publicized books including the best-selling *Brewing Up a Business*.[9]

At the heart of Dogfish Head's extraordinary success is its passion for innovation as well as for beer, and an ability to temper this out-of-the-box thinking and behavior with enough—but not *too* much—organization and discipline. The "Dogfish Way" of creating "off-centered ales for off-centered people" is about living life counterintuitively, against the grain. Dogfish Head's aim is not to vanquish the Big Two beer companies and their market domination. It is to define victory differently. It's a dream that doesn't only belong to Sam. "I believe in that dream," Cindy Houston, Dogfish's director of human resources, told us. And there are many more like her. Dogfish Head has been changing the face of the beer industry and etching out space for genuine creativity in a market characterized by standardization and uniformity.

However, Sam Calagione had overlooked one key fact when starting out: brewpubs were illegal in Delaware. So he had to begin his journey with a fight against the state where he successfully lobbied to pass a bill allowing restaurants to brew their own beer. Eventually, this stuttering start was turned into a great "origin myth" of how he once had to canoe beer illegally across the state line in order to get the brewpub up and running.

The early days of Dogfish Head were inauspicious. Sam was able to eke out a living from his food revenue while brewing small batches of exotic beer experimentally. He often slept on a mattress in the back room of his brewery to save costs and stay on task. Equipment was limited, scrapped together from items that others had discarded—which meant that he had to brew multiple batches of beer per day. But the brewpub's small size proved to be an unusual advantage: it meant that Sam could be experimental and innovative without risking great losses. If a batch was delicious, then customers would give it their assent— and Sam would just make some more. If it didn't succeed, little was wasted.

Sam's brewing team developed a strategy of putting ingredients into beer that had never been considered before—just to see how they would affect the taste. Dogfish Head beers typically contain unusual ingredients like saffron, chicory, Finnish juniper berries, and Antarctic water. These strange brews deliberately and boldly flout established tradition.

And yet, in creating new tastes for the future, Dogfish Head also makes innovative connections to the history of brewing in the past. Drawing on information about ancient Egyptian herbs acquired from an archaeologist, Dogfish Head created a *Midas Touch* brand that took its inspiration from a twenty-seven-hundred-year-old drink discovered in the tomb of King Midas. *Chateau Jiahu*, another Dogfish brand, is derived from a nine-thousand-year-old Chinese brew that is the oldest known alcoholic beverage.

Whether inspired by ancient brewing recipes from the past or by exotic ingredients of the present, Dogfish Head's extreme brewing pushes beer and the beer market to its limits. This against-the-grain approach is a lot of fun for the makers, and excellent business for the company. Nick Benz, who manages the accounts and oversees quality control points to how "People go 'Wow, look what they just did!'" At the same time, he said, the beer and the company itself is "still this fun, funky thing" that attracts people. "People gravitate towards things that are different," he observed. It's not, in his eyes, just about being "different for difference's sake." It's because "there's genuine intrinsic value in being different."

In truth, though, selecting ingredients isn't just a wild and chaotic process. As Nick emphasized, their goal is not to bottle unusual and eclectic ingredients merely *because* they are unusual and eclectic, but because they enhance the drinking experience for that particular style of beer. Dogfish also bases its choices on research and prior knowledge, and employs a disciplined and calculated brewing process. For example, Sam and the brewers study the sugar properties of particular fruits and yeasts to identify the ones that will complement various styles of beers. "Soft processes" of imaginative creation are combined with the hard data of rigorous research.

Nick Benz knows all about the dangers of being different for difference's sake. He is Sam Calagione's Number 2, describing himself as "the man behind" Calagione's larger-than-life figurehead. A prankster with a rebellious spirit, Sam was thrown out of high school before he found his way to college. His off-centered nature has made the company what it is—and he likes the people around him to be equally eccentric.

Sam's playful spirit is everywhere at Dogfish. All the people we spoke to were excited about their work. They are encouraged to play, have fun, and be creative. Sam's wife and company VP Mariah Calagione calls the atmosphere at Dogfish "controlled chaos" because there is usually something happening that appears slightly out of control. Yet she insists that this is positive, because it ensures that the team maintains their off-centered edge.

But surrounding yourself with people who reflect your own quirky character can only get you so far, and sometimes it can take you *too* far. Eventually, there is a tipping point where eccentricity turns into ineptitude. Ultimately, Dogfish's off-center attitude had to be tempered by organization and efficiency.

This is what business expert Jim Collins calls "disciplined innovation."[10] Like many other people, Collins understands that most innovations actually fail. Successful innovation doesn't just happen by throwing ideas around wildly and hoping for the best, or by abandoning them as soon as you get frustrated or lose interest. Successful innovators, Collins explains, are disciplined. "The great task, rarely achieved," he continues, "is to blend creative intensity with relentless discipline so as to amplify the creativity rather than destroy it."[11]

This is why Dogfish Head's board of directors, along with Mariah Calagione, pressed Sam to let go of the financial side of the brewery. Although he was excellent at drumming up business and improving the revenue stream, Sam was failing to manage that revenue internally—which he fully admits himself:

> Because I was bad at [managing] those things, we [were going to] stay unprofitable even if we kept growing. So it took our board, Mariah, and a bunch of smarter people than me on the cost side of running a business to say, "Sam, you're good at doing that revenue stuff but you've got to trust us [to be in charge of] getting more efficient and really paying attention to the expenses."

This is an area where Nick Benz has a good grip. When he arrived, the atmosphere at Dogfish was fun and funky—but there was a 30 percent failure rate at the bottling plant, and many workers were unskilled and incompetent. There were mad dashes to get beer to distributors, supply shortfalls at key points of the year, and poor checks on quality before the beer left the brewery. In Benz's recollection, it wasn't so much a business as "a hobby on steroids."

Because Nick and Sam are opposites, they didn't immediately attract. Sam is an eccentric and an iconoclast. Nick has a Carnegie-Mellon University MBA. Sam is a rebellious writer. Nick is an engineer. Their improbable match was not self-evidently made in heaven. Slowly, though, they each learned the value of what the other had to give. As Nick recalls:

> It took me probably 18 months of battles with Sam over the stupidest little things to teach him that not everything has to be so crazy, all punk, anarchistic, [or] chaotic—that there can be some order to what he does. But similarly there can be a hell of a lot less structure to the way that I think. We both came from very extreme positions and we both softened a bit off total

chaos and total organization to the point where we both respect and understand what each other brings to the table.

Nick and Sam set up a new bottling plant that "was properly designed and executed." Now, according to Nick, "you can actually think about what you're doing instead of having this rattling (noise) in your head." Dogfish benchmarked itself against other similarly placed breweries and found it was in the bottom third in wages and benefits. Mariah remembered how they would bring in people to "manage the restaurant until they'd burn out and they'd leave." Now, she says, Dogfish "pays well and has invested to build an entire management for the business."

As the hiring and staffing process became more professional, so did the accounting system. The business installed new data tracking systems that gave an accurate, detailed and timely picture of the company's costs to guide its business decisions. Nick Benz summed up their more disciplined strategy as "a three-part approach to improvement that involves a focus on good people, good data, and good decisions."

One result is that Sam has been able to concentrate on what he does best: being the eccentric face of the company with whom adventurous beer drinkers identify. "I know that my usefulness to this company is more in a cheerleader, evangelical, and educational capacity," Sam explained. "I am now able to focus more on the stuff that excites me about my work here than [I was] in the era when our company didn't have the financial wherewithal to hire the kind of talented people whose skills complement my own."

Dogfish Head Beer still maintains its cadre of quirky characters. But beneath the company's edgy surface image that brings in its enthusiastic customers, there is an undergirding structure of organization and efficiency that holds the whole business together. Nick Benz sums it all up as Sam is "the idea guy. I'm the guy that gets it done." Nick explained:

That diehard craft beer drinker is very fickle. If they think [you're getting] too big, you're a corporate sell-out—and the moment you start doing that, you alienate that base of diehard beer geeks, the people who got you where you are. So we're very conscious about the brand continuing to resonate with Sam and this funky, young, energetic, eclectic, fly-by-the-seat-of-your-pants, seemingly chaotic and almost anarchistic [face of], the company. [But internally], we're a very well-oiled machine.

Dogfish Head beer is an icon of counterintuitive thinking and action. It's a company that had to battle for new legislation to allow its idea to even come into existence. Its founder started up in his backroom by brewing beer that not even his friends thought they would like. Dogfish Head introduced beer ingredients that nobody else had thought of. Dogfish pulls customers toward it instead of pushing products on them. Beneath its innovative and anarchic veneer is a deeply disciplined approach to product development and business efficiency that maintains its "geeky" base while constantly putting out high quality product to ever-expanding numbers of customers. And in the end, Sam realized that as the company's formal leader and front man he didn't have to do it all himself, nor was it wise to surround himself only with people who performed in the quirky way that he did. High-performance leadership is about knowing your weaknesses as well as your strengths, about giving away areas of your power to those who can handle it better, and about building a team that can offset the liability of your limitations, even when they are lovably eccentric ones, and also complement your strengths.

When you do the unexpected, create something from nothing, and go against the grain, you will fail a lot. Dogfish had to endure a great deal of disappointment in order to succeed; but they eventually did this in a determined and disciplined way. So did Sir James Dyson. His vacuum cleaner, the Dyson, is now a household name. It revolutionized the way that house-cleaning was done, so that instead of hiding away disgusting dirt in an opaque bag, it made an entertaining spectacle of flying dirt in a transparent container. But before he had developed a successful prototype, Dyson produced 5,126 that failed. Yet he "learned from every one."[12] Dyson's advice for other creative innovators is that "You should admire the person who perseveres and slogs through and gets there in the end."[13]

Tom and David Kelley, the brothers who lead "design thinking" creator IDEO, conclude from their own work on creativity that to overcome failure, you not only have to confront and surmount your fears. You also "have to figure out what went wrong and what to do better next time." "If you don't," they say, "you're liable to repeat your errors in the future."[14]

In most areas, it's not enough to develop wacky innovations. It's also important that they work, that they make life better for the people who will use them. Saying, "I've learned so much when I've failed—I think I'll try it again" may be part of the answer to disciplined innovation. But it is *how* you try (and fail) as well as *how often* you try (and fail) that is the secret to securing innovative success.

Teach Less, Learn More

Improvement and innovation are different ways to bring about change. Improvement, on the one hand, is about getting better by increasing efficiency and effort in what you are already doing. It comes from working harder, putting in longer hours, eliminating errors, and galvanizing team effort. Innovation, on the other hand, requires that you change the game altogether. In this scenario, you improve by doing something completely new. Railways replacing the stagecoach, jet engines superseding propellers, and "video killing the radio star"[15] were all moments when disruptive innovation triumphed over incremental improvement. As Henry Ford said, "If I had asked people what they wanted, they would have said faster horses."[16]

There is a paradoxical relationship between improvement and innovation. When you have been improving by getting better at the same game, this is often when you need to change the game and do something different altogether. Decline tends to set in *before*, not right at the peak of performance. It takes place when performance is tailing off, but the numbers don't show it yet. This is a paradox of change. You have to know when to abandon and move on from the very thing that has been behind all your success.[17]

One country that has embraced this paradox is the tiny island nation of Singapore. When Singapore established independence from Malaysia in 1965, it was just a small former British colony of under a million people—a Third World country that TV naturalist David Attenborough described as just "a series of small tin sheds."[18] Within a generation and a half, under the determined leadership of Prime Minister Lee Kwan Yew, this "tiny red dot" of a nation—as a former President of Indonesia described it—achieved its inspiring dream of becoming an economically dynamic and highly developed nation.[19]

By 2011, Singapore had a population of well over five million (close to the size of some US states).[20] Its GDP per capita was in the world's top ten.[21] It had a startling economic growth rate of almost 15 percent per annum in 2010 and still around 5 percent in 2011 (compared to less than 2 percent in the United States and United Kingdom).[22] It was the world's top-performing country on the OECD's international tests of student achievement (PISA) in mathematics in 2012.[23] It is also a consistent high performer on other highly regarded tests in mathematics and science.[24] In addition, Singapore topped the highly competitive Asia Pacific region on the prestigious International Baccalaureate examination for the fourth year in a row in 2014, with high proportions of students achieving perfect scores.[25]

Singapore achieved this stunning success as early as the 1990s. A big part of the Singaporean economic boom was attributable to the achievement of the nation's schools. Singapore had raised its educational standards throughout the 1980s and early 1990s by introducing standardized testing, highly centralized control, a common curriculum, and intense competition between students and schools.[26] A combination of Eastern Confucian philosophy and British colonial history had created a culture of high expectations, hard work, respect for teachers and authority, perseverance, discipline, loyalty, and competitiveness. It was an approach that many lower-performing nations in the West then tried to emulate—and still do.

However, just when the West started to copy Singapore and other Asian high performers in education, these countries began moving in a different direction—toward more creativity in classroom learning, less centralized control of curriculum content, and more cooperation between schools to help each other improve their performance.[27] Why this turnaround, you might wonder? The main reason for this about-face in educational strategy is *economic competitiveness*.

In the early 1990s, Southeast Asia suffered a major financial collapse.[28] Rapidly developing economies such as Singapore's had built a lot of their growth on electronics manufacturing, by churning out parts for new Western products or assembling the products themselves. The emergence of new digital products exerted a crushing blow on many nations in the Southeast Asia electronics industry, including Singapore. The country's government was devastated. They became determined to ensure that nothing like that would ever happen again. Singapore's leaders realized their country would need to become a flexible, innovative, and high-performing knowledge economy, full of citizens with the skills to adapt and flex as the global economy required. And the place to begin—indeed, the only place that a tiny nation without natural resources could go—was education.

Instead of rote learning and memorizing content, Singapore realized that its students would need to learn how to be innovative, apply knowledge to unfamiliar problems, and think critically about the information presented to them. Instead of having only moderately capable teachers who would teach the prescribed curriculum, the country would need to attract highly qualified teachers by offering them starting salaries equivalent to what engineers were making. And instead of having schools engaged in win-lose competition where they kept the secrets of their success to themselves, they would need to share their knowledge for the good of the entire nation. The strategies that had gotten Singapore to where it was by the early to mid-1990s would not be sufficient to carry it into the twenty-first century.

It was with these thoughts in mind that Prime Minister Goh Chok Tong launched the country's new vision of flexibility and innovation with the inspiring slogan of *Thinking Schools, Learning Nation*. This new direction was meant to develop "thinking and committed citizens" who would drive the nation forward to an even more dynamic future.[29]

Seven years later, the strategy turned into a paradoxically titled initiative called *Teach Less, Learn More*. During the 2004 National Day Rally, Singapore's Prime Minister Lee Hsien Loong declared that "we have to teach less to our students so that they will learn more."[30] He wanted children to be prepared for the "test of life," not a "life of tests."[31] And if students were going to become innovative, then their teachers would have to be able to innovate as well. So the nation took steps to allocate roughly 20 percent of school time for educators to design their own classroom lessons with their own curriculum content. At the same time, schools would be organized in clusters to learn from each other.

The *Teach Less, Learn More* initiative's goal wasn't just to crank out higher test scores; it was about developing higher-quality learning among students. The policy underscored the fact that students don't learn anything of great quality if instructors are merely telling them more things, more often. The "teaching less" approach isn't about lowering standards or doing less work. It involves finding out what truly engages students, constructing real problems that stimulate their commitment and imagination, and structuring their learning so they will think critically and inquire into problems themselves—rather than learning the answer directly from the front of the class.

The power of *Teach Less, Learn More* is evident in the way that some Singaporean schools are starting to use digital and online technologies to stimulate and support student learning.[32] One of these, Ngee Ann Secondary School, started up just about the time that *Thinking Schools, Learning Nation* did, in 1995. Within fifteen years, it has become a national and world leader in technology-enhanced learning. Ngee Ann has been showcased in videos produced by the George Lucas Foundation and by the Organization for Economic Cooperation and Development. It was recognized by Microsoft as one of only thirty-three selected schools in the world that have successfully incorporated technology into learning, and its staff members have won numerous national awards.

Until 2013, Adrian Lim was the school's dynamic young principal. Despite all the awards that Ngee Ann Secondary has received for innovative digital technology (called Information & Communication Technology or ICT for short), Adrian and his staff maintain that good teaching "must lead technology and not the other way round. We don't use ICT for every single lesson," Adrian says. "At the end of the day, the fundamentals [anchor us]—where a good teacher engages students in class and they make the subject come alive. ICT is not the silver bullet."

Technology has become a mere fad in some schools and systems across the world, with dubious and sometimes disastrous results for students' learning. School districts stack up their schools with electronic tablets that become little more than fancy note-taking devices. Interactive whiteboards are used no differently than old-fashioned chalkboards. In too many cases, technology drives the teaching and merely distracts the students. At Ngee Ann, though, it works the other way around: technology stimulates good teachers to become even better.

For instance, Ngee Ann has taken a counterintuitive approach to students' use of smart phones. In the United States and many other countries, teachers ban student smartphones in the classroom, viewing them—quite naturally—as distractions. Ngee Ann Secondary, however, sees smartphones as teaching and learning tools. They allow students to use Twitter as a feedback device. This gives shy students a way to record their responses to their learning and to get involved in class discussion. It provides teachers with data about their students' learning that they can review after class and sometimes as the class is happening. Students are also "more engaged because they are using something they are very familiar with and very good at," Adrian Lim explained. Students still sometimes misuse phones, of course, but Adrian Lim just confiscated their "best phones" for a day or two and replaced them with an older model substitute to get their attention, rather than prohibiting them entirely.

Ngee Ann has also bought an island in the popular simulation *Second Life* where it has created a virtual art gallery. This enables more students to display more artwork than the school's physical space will allow. They have also shared this work with art from an aboriginal community in Australia. Second Life's simulation capabilities also allow students to walk inside and look around famous paintings from different perspectives. Normally, Adrian Lim said, when students are asked what they think about a painting, they "start covering their heads. But when you put it in their world, everybody seems to have their opinion about 'what is this art piece?'" At Ngee Ann, technology is a part of good teaching, not a substitute for it.

A number of countries in Asia are becoming innovative trailblazers in education reform today. In contrast, many Western countries are still trying to do more of the testing and centralized prescription of teaching—and learning—that the East is quickly leaving behind. Singapore knew it had to innovate during the mid-1990s, even though it already topped the world on the conventional tests of educational achievement that preceded the use of PISA ten years later. It is using technology to strengthen good teaching, not to displace or downgrade it. And it is gradually relaxing the old top-down controls of central bureaucracies in favor of promoting greater flexibility and supporting schools to assist and learn from each other.

Entranced Not Entrenched

When Angela Ahrendts became CEO of the 150-year-old British Burberry company in 2006, she realized the luxury apparel firm had lost its focus. She noticed something unusual as she watched her top executives arrive at her first summit: "They had flown in from around the world to classic British weather, gray and damp, but not one of these 60 people was wearing a Burberry trench coat." She wondered if any of them even *owned* one, and reasoned, "If our top people weren't buying our [own] products, despite the great discount they could get, how could we expect *customers* to pay full price for them?"[33]

The company was founded in 1856 by twenty-one-year-old former draper's assistant Thomas Burberry.[34] He branded the gabardine, a hard-wearing, waterproof, and breathable fabric that was perfectly suited to the British climate. In 1911, Burberry clothed Roald Amundsen, the first person to reach the South Pole; and George Mallory was last seen heading for the top of Everest in 1924 wearing a Burberry jacket. Long Burberry coats protected British army officers in the trenches during World War I.

Of course, this is very different from today when graceful models glide along catwalks in stylish Burberry trench coats. And the 2013 design collection was modeled by ten-year-old Romeo Beckham.

But Midwesterner Ahrendts had a tough time bringing this aristocratic company back to focus on its core brand. Ahrendts' appointment surprised many in the British establishment. What could someone raised in small-town Indiana possibly know about running a company which, by Royal Appointment, made clothing for Her Majesty the Queen?

They would soon find out. When Ahrendts arrived in 2006, Burberry was growing at a glacial 2 percent in a rapidly expanding global market of luxury goods. By the end of 2013, its annual operating profit had risen by over 17 percent.[35] It was no surprise, then, that Burberry was the fastest-growing luxury brand on Interbrand's index in 2012.[36]

Two counter-flow strategies played a part in this remarkable makeover. First was the way that Ahrendts brought the company back to focus on its core brand—the trench coat. Burberry had licensed its brand to twenty-three sites around the world and encouraged diversity as the best way to capture as much market share as possible. As she visited these sites, Ahrendts discovered all kinds of apparel with the famous Burberry check: kilts, polo shirts, even dog's coats and leashes. There was nothing wrong with the products; they were just *too diverse*. Ahrendts recalls how "together they added up to just a lot of stuff—something for everybody, but none of it exclusive or compelling."[37]

Ahrendts admires and respects great brands. She loves trusting and knowing that whatever country you visit, you will have the same great service and products when you shop at your favorite store or taste the same drink in the same container. And she felt that Burberry was missing this. When she reached Hong Kong—another locale that gets more than its fair share of rain—she found that while the design team had everything in check, there was not a single trench coat in sight.

Ahrendts realized that Burberry wasn't capitalizing on its historical core business—its heritage and its unique luxury brand. At first, as with many counterintuitive dreamers, some of Ahrendts' colleagues were far from convinced about the apparent back-to-basics approach that focused on the trench coat. "Some managers were cynical," she recalled. "A lot of them had been at Burberry for a really long time, [and] I'm sure they left saying, 'Focusing on trench coats—*that's* our strategy?'"

"However," Ahrendts continued, "most of us were confident that it was the right plan." Burberry was connecting its inspiring designer future to the best of its heritage in the past. The decision to focus on the trench coat unleashed a wave of creative talent guided by designer Christopher Bailey. Ahrendts and Bailey had worked together before, so they shared mutual trust and instinctive understanding. Ahrendts introduced Bailey as the brand czar and told the team, "Anything that the consumer sees—anywhere in the world—will go through his office. No exceptions."[38] The result is that, in addition to the classic beige, Burberry now sells trench coats in a range of entrancing colors with accoutrements such as alligator epaulets and mink collars.

The second counter-flow strategy involved Burberry's approach to the luxury market. It was competing in one of the world's fastest-growing sectors, particularly in China. Burberry adopted a groundbreaking inclusive approach through social media, by targeting the luxury customers of the future—the Millennials. This was a completely different way of dealing with customers than had been customary with most luxury brands who had established an elitist and exclusive reputation that was not so much uplifting as almost out of reach. In contrast, Burberry has positioned social media at the heart of its business. By 2012, it became the world's most successful luxury brand on Facebook with ten million fans and seven hundred thousand followers on Twitter.[39] And by 2014 these grew to seventeen million Facebook fans and 2.85 million Twitter followers.

Back in the trenches, Ahrendts had a fight on her hands. She released the entire design team in Hong Kong, shut down the New

Jersey factory, brought some of the US design team to London and closed a three-hundred-employee factory making polo shirts in Wales. The Welsh move caused an outcry and Ahrendts was hauled into Parliament to answer questions from government ministers.[40] But she remained resolute throughout, and knew she had to make these difficult decisions so that Burberry could invest in its Yorkshire factory—and double the workforce that wove the high-quality yarn into Burberry trench coats.

Kathy Gersch, executive vice president at international strategy firm Kotter International, summarizes Burberry's makeover by emphasizing how "it took not just Ahrendts, but all of Burberry to make this turnaround happen. She painted a clear picture of the opportunity for the company. She ensured everyone understood the vision. Then, she engaged the organization in helping to accomplish it." Gersch explains that "Ahrendts retrained her sales people by bringing multi-media re-education programs to each store. But she didn't just direct them how to sell. She also shared the 'why': that the trench coat is unique to Burberry; it's core to the brand." Crucially, "she empowered the sales staff to become a powerful force of brand advocates."

Ahrendts uplifted Burberry from the trenches with its trenches. She shared a clear and compelling vision throughout the company that counterintuitively connected Burberry's chic future to its classic past. She brought drive and determination to this quest by eliminating the unfocused branding and ineffective work practices of the recent past and by making an exclusive high-end product widely available to the customers of the future on social media. By combining new creative talent with its classically British image, she restored the company as one of the world's leading luxury brands and reached out to a burgeoning global market of affluent young customers, especially in Asia. Ahrendts leaves Burberry in good shape as she heads off in 2014 to enhance another global brand as leader of the retail empire at mighty Apple.[41]

Conclusion

In times of crisis, uplifting leaders often do the exact opposite of what others might expect or anticipate. They are unconventional and counterintuitive thinkers who know how to be imaginative and resourceful in adverse and volatile conditions. They have a remarkable ability to size up a difficult situation before taking bold steps to advance forward. They tend to be relentlessly optimistic even in the face of evidence that demonstrates the sheer extent of the challenge or the unlikelihood of success. Like Singapore's prime minister, who told his nation's schools to teach less if they wanted their students to learn more, they seem to defy the logic of their country's or organization's history. Or like Angela Ahrendts at Burberry, they can mystify their colleagues at first, by returning to but also reinventing an apparently outmoded product that their company seemed to have long since abandoned.

Uplifting leaders know how to develop creative cultures that take risks. At Dogfish Head Craft Brewery, constant innovation in product is the "fun, funky" thing that keeps employees motivated and keeps attracting customers. They know how to see elements often regarded as negatives in a positive light—in much the same way that teachers at Ngee Ann Secondary School don't view smartphones as an annoying disruption to classroom teaching but rather as useful teaching tools that are integral to almost all students' lives. And Apple has welcomed and nurtured ideas like touch-screen technology—which their competitors perceived as peripheral or crazy—seeing them as the potential next big thing. These organizations know that their survival depends on someone taking a different route, finding an alternative perspective, and creating a completely novel product or approach.

However, if all you have is creativity, innovation can quickly turn into self-indulgence and chaos. When autonomy and innovation were all that defined the early culture of Dogfish Head, staff became unreliable and quality collapsed. Singapore has promoted more innovation among its teachers, but it has not abolished accountability at the same time. Autonomy need not turn into chaos as long as it's balanced with a sense of disciplined collective responsibility. This comes from having a shared dream, pursuing it with determination, appointing leaders with complementary skills that offset those of impassioned innovators, and forging a common identity that binds the whole community together. Soft processes and hard-nosed accountability can and do work together. These unusual attractions of opposites are especially apparent in the juxtaposition of competition and collaboration—the subject of our next chapter.

Chapter Three

Collaboration with Competition

With Salli Humphreys

Friendships born on the field of athletic strife are the real gold of competition.
Awards become corroded, friends gather no dust.

—Jesse Owens

Opposites Attract

Among all the counterintuitive ways to bring about change, to create something from nothing, or turn failure into success, changing the way we think about the traditional relationship between collaboration and competition is one of the most powerful. It comes as no surprise that the two are often seen and defined as opposites. Some people believe that humans are by nature selfish; others believe we're cooperative. It is said that competition makes us succeed to survive or to be superior. Cooperation, by contrast, harnesses our collective talents and abilities to succeed together.

Opposing and contradictory opinions about collaboration and competition are widespread. People hold profoundly different beliefs about whether human nature is basically cooperative and motivated by the common good or competitive and driven by self-interest. A number of classic management theories have been founded on these separate premises. Competition and collaboration define and delineate the ideological differences between capitalism and socialism. They distinguish between winning at all costs, and believing that collective victory is what truly matters. In some countries, parents and schools compete fiercely to secure the best education possible for their children. In others, the focus is on educating *all* young people in the community for the common public good.

In some cases, competition and collaboration are not just opposites; they're enemies. In sports, investing resources in elite competitive teams at the expense of broader participation can reduce the pool of talent on which these teams are able to draw. And schools that devote energy to competing with each other aren't able to mobilize and circulate knowledge about good professional practices that might improve the system as a whole.

Cooperation can also undermine competition. Collaboration and attachments to community can become obstacles to the flexible movement of skills and labor in business. When a company pursues social causes even at the expense of making a profit, it can undercut its basic capacity to exist and to make social contributions in the future. Advocates of less competition and more participation in school sports are likewise criticized for undermining the will to win.

However, the relationship between collaboration and competition needn't be a *zero-sum* game; one doesn't have to prevail at the expense of the other. Collaboration and competition can and do work well together in productive ways—something that's not only desirable but also increasingly essential in today's complex, global marketplace.

Half a century ago, Harvard psychologist David McClelland developed one of the most profound theories of human motivation since Herbert Maslow's famous hierarchy of needs. McClelland explained that people in business and other organizations are driven to perform and produce by one or more of three different needs.[1]

- Those with a high *need for achievement* are **driven to excel**. They benefit from feedback as well as from working in environments that challenge and stretch them, and they enjoy either working alone or with fellow high achievers.
- Those with a high *need for affiliation* are drawn to **collaborative working environments**, enjoy relationships with others, and need to be accepted by the group. They perform well in areas like sales and human resources, and make good process consultants.
- Those who are driven by a *need for power* are either **drawn to exercise power** and dominance over others personally, or, more usefully, **pulled toward using social power**—achieving the goals of the community by exercising their power with and through those around them.

The need for dominance and achievement tends to drive competitiveness. The needs for affiliation and social power are more in tune with the collaborative spirit. But in the fast-moving, globalized environment of relentless change and ever-extending networks, we must now address these needs simultaneously. Leaders today must know how to keep on lifting up performance, stay ahead of the competition, challenge themselves and their colleagues relentlessly, and continue searching for the next advantage and innovative breakthrough that can move them further forward. At the same time, they also need to access all the information and insight they can get to inform their efforts and elevate their achievements. They must benchmark their practice against similar organizations, constantly learn about what their competitors are doing, network locally and globally for new ideas, and seek out partnerships and alliances with individuals and organizations who can help them to compete, contribute, and progress.

There are already a number of ways in which collaboration and competition, and the needs that drive them, come together:

1. Collaboration can *compensate* for the excesses of competition. For example, philanthropists and social reformers in nineteenth-century Britain and America introduced civic projects such as public health, the first public schools, and the great municipal parks to rebuild communities and offset capitalism's most destructively competitive effects.

2. Collaboration can *complement* the forces of competition. Group effort and allegiance to an internal team can increase people's external competitive edge against other teams. For instance, in their account of the human resource strategy at Whole Foods market in the United States, which they discuss in their book *Conscious Capitalism*, John MacKey and Raj Sisodia describe how Whole Foods rejected the legendary approach of CEO Jack Welch at GM in the 1980s in which the bottom 10 percent of staff were fired every year.[2] Whole Foods CEO Mackey felt that this "creates a climate of fear" that "pits people against one another."[3] So instead, Whole Foods builds teams that support, engage, motivate, reward, and even vet each other—and if everyone does well, *everyone* stays! Even so, teams still compete against teams in other stores or regions and feel pride in their performance when they win. In the words of Mackey and Sisodia, Welch's model encourages "team members [to] compete not to be terminated," while in Whole Foods', "they compete as part of a team to be rewarded, but no-one is necessarily cut."[4]

3. Collaboration and competition can also strike a *compromise* in which all parties get some, but not all, of what they want. The

corporate social responsibility movement has compelled companies to pay attention to the communities in which they are located and the environments that they affect.[5] Systemwide regulations limit the ability of many wealthy sports organizations to plunder talent from lesser clubs through measures such as draft pick procedures, wage caps, and squad size limits. Regulatory frameworks can also require schools that compete with each other to take a full and representative range of students, creating fairer competition as a result.

Uplifting leaders know how to go beyond the ideological opposites of collaboration and competition and have them work together in complementary, compensatory, and compromising ways. But our research also reveals that uplifting organizations and their leaders know how to go further than this through counterintuitive fusions of collaboration and competition that create

- *Increased value*—in overall performance and outcomes
- *New value*—fresh accomplishments that people cannot achieve alone
- *Social value*—by advancing a greater moral good for the wider community
- *Motivational value*—through the energizing thrill that people get from outdoing each other and from improving on their own performance along the way

Counterintuitive fusions of competition and collaboration are evident among close rivals who work together for mutual interest and greater good in sports. Direct competitors create new products together in business. Similarly, neighboring schools in the same market for local students can and sometimes do collaborate to help each other serve the common good of their community.

Co-opetition

Fierce competition is an essential prerequisite for success in sports organizations. Unless teams are driven by a powerful desire to beat their opponents, they will end up as losers and this will drag them down. So you might wonder why you would ever help your competitors. But that's exactly what a number of the uplifting teams in our study actually did.

Most US sports fans find the game of cricket to be incomprehensible and dull; comedian Robin Williams once described it as "baseball on valium."[6] But in other countries, like India, cricket is the leading competitive sport. And in a business-driven, media-aware, sporting environment, it's adopting increasingly exciting formats and reaching an ever-expanding global market.

In 2008–2009, the world cricket rankings had been repeatedly topped by Australia, ranked Number 1 in both men's and women's cricket.[7] Inside Melbourne Cricket Ground, the amphitheater of Australian cricket, we sat down with Malcolm Speed, former chief executive of the International Cricket Council. It was like having an audience with a sporting god, since Speed was his sport's global equivalent of the US Commissioner of Baseball.[8]

However, Speed faced his share of human error when he was appointed as the CEO of Cricket Australia in 1997. There was pervasive "player unrest," with players becoming embroiled in highly publicized scandals, along with a "war over payments." A strike seemed likely if players' contracts and salaries didn't improve. Speed explained that the situation was "very public" and "quite ugly." The Australian cricket team had led the world for a decade. Now it seemed destined for disruption and decline.

But Malcolm Speed was not one to shy away from a challenge. In his twenty years as a "club cricketer," he had been the sport's equivalent of a curveball pitcher in baseball. Speed had always preferred to "bowl up the hill, into the wind" to make the ball swing about. And his approach to management was no different.

Speed was a lawyer with prior experience of high-level sports administration for Basketball Australia. He knew he could not increase player professionalism and eradicate corrosive resentments without a stronger financial structure that would make cricket salaries more attractive compared to those in other Australian sports that were competing for the same athletic talent. Previously, Cricket Australia's income had been divided equally between sponsorships, gate receipts, and media revenue. But during Speed's leadership a new model started to evolve in which, over a ten-year period, about 70 percent of the income eventually came from global media rights. This increased overall revenue and made it possible to create a better financial reward structure for the players.

The redesigned pay structures meant that players enjoyed an improved relationship with the team. A new player contract system introduced rankings related to individual performance and future potential as well as value to the team. Players were now paid under a more transparent system.

Speed's strategy was counterintuitive—not so much in generating more income for players, but in identifying *where* that income would come from. Much of the income from media revenue would come from one country—India; one of Australia's *major competitors*. Managerially, Speed had redefined the relationship between collaboration and competition. To use his own words, he had "bowled uphill into the wind" and "got more swing that way."

"The deals were done, 2000, 2001 and 2002 for those increased media rights," Speed explained, "but they did not take effect until after I'd gone." Dan Markham was the energetic, quick-talking general manager of media rights at Cricket Australia at the time of our study.[9] Because he'd come from the English Premier League of soccer, Markham knew all about global media markets. He was one of the key people responsible for implementing Speed's financial vision by dramatically rethinking Australia's relationship with India.

India, Markham explained, was "the financial power"—"the unique selling point" of world cricket. So it was crucial, he said, to have Australia and India playing each other as often as possible. This also meant that—in both cricketing and cultural terms—it was essential "to keep India as strong as possible, keep tours to and from India occurring, and tap into that emerging economy."

A big part of Dan Markham's job was to maximize benefits and minimize risks. In practice, this meant lobbying the Australian and Indian governments for legislative changes to promote a better media environment. Counterintuitively, it also meant investing in India's community and cricketing development. For instance, Australia supplied India and other cricketing nations like Sri Lanka and Bangladesh with a lot of its own coaching expertise.

Cricket Australia believes they are making a morally worthwhile contribution to community development, helping to create a more stable social and political environment, and also producing stronger Indian teams that can provide keen and commercially attractive competition. Cricket Australia's strategy generates increased financial and performance value, stronger social value, and greater motivational value. As Markham put it:

> From a media perspective, stronger, closer contests make more compelling viewing. No one wants to see a complete, one-sided, foregone conclusion of an event. Let's not forget: India is our economic driver. So a terrible Indian team creates terrible results for us. [In this way,] actually helping the Indian team leads to better contests, better revenue, and a better economic situation.

Cricket Australia, in other words, sleeps with its enemy. It collaborates with one of its leading adversaries in order to develop that opponent's capacity and competitiveness. This innovative approach would have been a bold step where any partner was concerned. But the risks associated with India were especially intense at the time the strategy was initiated. The country was vulnerable to political instability and insecurity. India never toured Australia at all during the 1990s. When India played Pakistan on Australian soil in the early years of Malcolm Speed's leadership, the two countries were still at war in Kashmir.

The more traditional members of the board of directors at Cricket Australia were skeptical about investing in competitors—especially those as ridden with risk as India. They were concerned that this type of generosity would undermine Australia's own capacity for winning, that collaboration would threaten competition. But leaders in other parts of the organization understood the commercial and competitive benefits to be gained from this unusual arrangement. This intensified the motivational value of close competition between teams and developed increased commercial value accruing to the organization. In general, Cricket Australia now understands that "you have to grow the game nationally by growing it internationally."[10]

Dan Markham felt that there had been "a real danger of Australia becoming too good." As he explains: "I think sports suffer if somebody is so much better than anybody else; people start to lose interest." Supporting the development of other countries meant that teams became more closely packed together in terms of their winning potential, which kept all of them performing at the highest standard. And in the end, although tighter contests and better games have occasionally led to India outplaying Australia, this has still meant that more viewers have tuned in, growing global media revenue as they did so.

Markham referred to this overall approach as *co-opetition*—"cooperating with your competition to your benefit"—a term that originated in the business world in 1996. In their book

Co-opetition, Harvard and Yale Professors Adam Brandenburger and Barry Nalebuff based their concept of co-opetition on game theory.[11] Exponents of game theory regard winner-takes-all competition as a *zero-sum* game because the total amount to play for at the start of the game is the same at the end, when the loser ends up with nothing. By comparison, co-opetition is a *plus-sum* game: it creates more value as it is played and those involved end up with more than the combined total they had at the start. Co-opetition in business actually increases the market for which you compete. Even if you keep the same shares of the market, everyone wins.

Partnerships and consortia are normal practice in business these days. A 2006 survey of 187 senior executives by the Economist Intelligence Unit found that all but 5 percent of them were involved in collaborative relationships with corporate partners.[12] But co-opetition ratchets these partnerships up to a new level by involving direct and sometimes bitter rivals. One example is the European Airbus Consortium, which brought together not only competing companies but also the competing governments behind them.[13] In the United States, one explanation for the movement of the center of gravity for technology firms from the Boston area to Silicon Valley starting in the 1970s was that the New England businesses protected their company secrets by preventing employees talking to rival firms, whereas their California competitors encouraged more openness and networking between companies to move knowledge and innovation around.[14]

For more than a decade, a growing number of companies have realized the necessity of developing strategic alliances and partnerships—sometimes on a global scale. When you can collect and cash in frequent-flyer points on multiple airlines and hotels with the same account, you are participating in a strategic alliance for mutual benefit.

Fiat Auto exemplifies these more advanced forms of strategic alliance. In a world of increasing consolidation within the auto industry, Fiat's main competition is with other large manufacturers. Yet this does not prohibit the brand from interacting with, learning from, and even actively partnering with key competitors in order to produce components that are easier and cheaper to purchase from each other than having to make them all by themselves. For example, as Fiat's CEO Sergio Marchionne explains, "What is the point of one guy developing a 1.3 engine and another guy a 1.4? What are you getting for this? The answer is nothing: a total waste of capital."[15] Fiat and other manufacturers' competitive edge now depends not on how long it takes them to produce their own components—but in how efficiently they can assemble these components into a vehicle.

Uplifting Federations

Co-opetition does serve mutual interest, but it involves more than horse-trading or quid pro quos. As Rosabeth Moss Kanter told us in the 1990s, this combination of collaboration and competition creates new and enhances existing value.[16] But it also does something that is arguably even greater than this: co-opetition *creates transcendent value among and beyond all participants.* This is the value of something higher in aesthetic taste or moral purpose that competitors want to advance together.

When Dogfish Head CEO Sam Calagione—whom we first introduced in chapter 2—appeared on morning TV, he could simply have touted his own beers. But he also rooted for the success of other smaller brewers who, in many ways, were his immediate competitors. While promoting his popular book, *He Said Beer, She Said Wine*, he showcased one beer from Dogfish and also one from New Belgium Brewing.[17] This bolstered their shared identity as quality craft beers, rather than pitting them against each other in win-lose competition.

Sam does not feel envy if the media spotlight does not fall directly on Dogfish. "You'll never see me pissed off that somebody in my community got a great article written about them and it didn't get written about Dogfish, because I know a rising tide raises all ships and I want to see all small breweries succeed." Sam clearly appreciates co-opetition; but he also knows it's bigger than that. Co-opetition is about adding social value to the idea of small business, independence, and elevated taste: "I really believe there's a lot of good karma in my celebrating other small breweries I believe in, and not just Dogfish Head."

Sam's books include stories of other breweries and beers. When he hosts a beer dinner, he usually features non-Dogfish beers as well. He believes that Dogfish's own attempts to grow cannot come at the expense of its peers. The prominent position that Dogfish occupies in the media enables it to build a strong network of small breweries that can collectively compete against their much more powerful rivals in the three largest beer corporations. There's more to this than the other microbreweries being their enemies' enemy. It encourages the shared passion for great tasting beer and for the sheer chutzpah of underdogs all banding together against the Big Two.

In 2009, Dogfish took its work with improbable collaborators one step further when it partnered with Sierra Nevada Ales, a major competitor, to launch a new, alternative beer together. Their uplifting higher purpose was to promote the social value of independent craft-brewing in general. Good karma, raising all boats, shared independence, continuous innovation, and good taste—Dogfish valued all these things and continued to produce more beer and more diverse beers in the process.

In education, the fusion of competition and collaboration has taken some even more striking and also successful forms. Schools don't only collaborate and cooperate as they did in the California Teachers' Association project; they even work together in a competitive environment of market-based initiatives such as charter schools in the United States, free schools in Sweden, and academies in the United Kingdom. One of the points of origin of how to create collaborative relations among schools that compete is London, England.

Like the borough of Burnley, the London borough of Hackney is among the most deprived communities in England.[18] During the 1990s it was constantly featured in the national media for all the wrong reasons. For example, the closure of a failing secondary school incurred high profile protests from famous alumni like international movie star Michael Caine.[19] In addition to this unwanted media attention, Hackney Council's budget went into a tailspin of deficits from £3m to £65m from 1998 to 2000, putting it on the brink of bankruptcy.[20]

In the midst of all this, the borough's council members were at constant loggerheads with the government and the public, as well as being bitterly divided among themselves. "Our fingers are not on the pulse of the borough, but on each other's throats," one of them told the press.[21] In 1999, the UK government's Minister for Schools declared Hackney to be "the worst LEA (school district) in the country."[22] The district's children were in double jeopardy: not only did they live in a profoundly disadvantaged community, but they were also being educated in a deeply dysfunctional school system.

Tony Blair's government tried many familiar top-down and market-driven solutions to turn around the borough that had become a constant embarrassment on the doorstep of Parliament. It forced the council to accept something called the Hackney Improvement Team; however, this was instantly and infamously dubbed the HIT squad, guaranteeing that it had minimal positive effect. Hackney's School Improvement and Ethnic Minority services were then placed in the hands of a private company that proved to be bureaucratically inaccessible, could not build local capacity, and attracted media criticism for making profits at the expense of the poorest community in England.[23]

In 2002, the government came up with the somewhat creative idea of transferring the administration of the entire Hackney education department to a private nonprofit company called The

Learning Trust under a ten-year contract.[24] The Trust's only interest was in the achievements of the borough's children. It reported to a board of nonexecutive directors that included members of the council, the community, and the schools. And it had a decade to make a sustainable change, including rebuilding the capacity of the seventy-three-school system that educates thirty-six thousand students.

The Trust's work produced remarkable results. In an ethnically diverse community of almost a quarter of a million residents who spoke over a hundred languages between them—and who lived on very low incomes—Hackney schools were beating the national averages on all achievement tests by 2012. How did the Trust achieve this?

One explanation is that leaders of the Trust, like its chair, Sir Mike Tomlinson, believed that wherever possible, "the solution has got to come from within Hackney." One of its officers remembered how the Trust made the initial mistake of relying too much on external consultants, many of them from the private sector who remained after the earlier, unsuccessful, outsourcing.

> A lot of these people came in with a negative attitude. They regarded people who had worked in Hackney for many years as incompetent, inefficient, not knowing what they were doing. The irony is [the people who believed that] didn't last long here. It's the people who have worked here for a long time who have made the difference.

One of the Trust's more controversial moves was to build five new secondary school academies—similar to US charter schools.[25] Organizing public education on the principles of competitive markets between individual schools, without local control, in a bid for parent customers, has often created cultures that focus on "my child," "my class," and "my school"—with no thought for anyone else's child, class, or school. So the Hackney Learning Trust insisted that the academies protect and strengthen Hackney's educational community—not undermine it. Mike Tomlinson recalled that the schools "had to be non-selective and a member of the family of Hackney schools." He added, "We didn't want those who became islands unto themselves, or those who wouldn't cooperate."

The point was to ensure that people should have an allegiance to Hackney's community, and its children—to a purpose that was bigger than their own self-interest. Tomlinson recalled how "the Trust told the head teachers [UK's term for a school principal] that they had to work to the common good: '[Even though you're] head of one school, you have a collective responsibility for every young person in Hackney. [You can't] simply send all your difficult pupils to one school.'" Challenging students therefore became a *shared responsibility*. To fulfill these principles of collective accountability, educators established support networks among the borough's primary schools to help each other when anyone was struggling. National government policy supported these school-to-school networks, called *federations*—but it was up to Hackney to figure out how to make them work.

Two of the system's leaders developed Hackney's first federation. In 2004, test scores dropped at Holy Trinity Primary School in Hackney, the school failed an external inspection, the head teacher resigned, and the school was left high and dry with little idea about how to improve. Tricia Okoruwa, deputy director of The Learning Trust at the time, didn't adopt the usual strategies of sending in a turnaround team or closing down the school. Instead, she turned to the head of St. John & St. James Primary School, Siân Davies, who had successfully raised her school from the relics of a failing school with the same children in the same buildings.[26]

At first, there was no grand design to create a federation. The priority was to repair learning and teaching at Holy Trinity.

So Okoruwa and Davies agreed that Davies would run both her own school and Holy Trinity. They created a strategic alliance between the schools and established a new role of executive principal of both schools for Davies.

They saw immediate benefits. As leader of both schools, Davies could switch teachers from St. John & St. James to coach their counterparts at Holy Trinity, or show teachers from Holy Trinity examples of good teaching in St. John & St. James. Within just twelve months, inspectors proclaimed that Holy Trinity was a good school.[27] The schools and their staffs now shared common values, teaching practices, and a commitment to continue working together for the benefit of their students.

One risk of school-to-school federations is burnout among able and willing school leaders who take on too much. Leadership must be distributed sideways and shared more widely with appropriate support.[28] This was an attractive situation for young, talented, and ambitious teachers. Some of the routine leadership responsibilities in each school were therefore transferred from the head's office to other staff. With additional government resources provided by the federation initiative, Davies promoted two trusted and respected teacher leaders to become heads of school in Holy Trinity and St. John & St. James, respectively. Other teacher leaders were given responsibility for improving teaching and learning across the federation. Yvonne Barnett, now head teacher at Holy Trinity, remembers that rapid growth occurred because they worked so well together and knew the same systems. "We had consistently high expectations and we very clearly shared the same vision." The schools were eventually joined in a formal federation under one governing body with Davies as executive principal.

When another school failed its inspection, Okoruwa asked Davies if the federation would take it on—and the same remarkable turnaround ensued. Their federation has since uplifted several failing schools that are now all well on their way to being officially classified as outstanding. Under Davies' leadership as executive principal, the federation comprised six schools by 2014.[29] Some heads of the schools have in turn moved on to launch other federations in Hackney, stepping up to become executive principals themselves, and extending leadership around them so that the improvement efforts will be sustainable.

The results speak for themselves. Hackney now performs well above the national average on all key indicators of achievement. In 2012, ten trailblazing students from Hackney schools won places at Cambridge and Oxford universities, England's equivalent of the Ivy League, followed by thirteen more in 2013. This was the first time in decades that anyone from Hackney had even dreamt of going to these elite colleges, let alone making the grades to get there. Ninety percent of staff across the borough would recommend Hackney to others as a "good place to work." Parents outside the borough are struggling to get their children into all of Hackney's oversubscribed schools. Alan Wood, former chief executive of The Learning Trust, recalls how, "The Learning Trust stopped the madness and created an education system that people feel part of and proud of. Pupils, teachers, head teachers and governors all say what The Learning Trust did was to come in, get hold of it and sort it out. We removed history and that baggage. We made it clear how important education is. We have created a platform where there are no excuses now, absolutely none. Nobody can blame the local authority, or teachers or poor recruitment. Nobody can blame the kids. We've proved that schools in places like Hackney can do as well as schools anywhere."

The system isn't foolproof, of course. Research on other federations of English schools shows that some simply talk about ideas but fail to enact them when left to their own devices. And others that are forced to collaborate are too awkward and contrived to get results. But Hackney is not alone. Strong federations with clear structures of shared leadership, transparent participation, and collective responsibility for outcomes *do* raise achievement by having strong schools and leaders help weaker partners.[30]

These approaches to change are slow to take root in the United States. Neighboring public schools and charter schools are usually in win-lose competitions with each other for students and sheer survival. Some schools and teachers may network with each other to share experiences or ideas, but they do not take joint responsibility for mutual success. Other schools work together within the same chain or "brand" of charter schools, but they do not collaborate within and for the same community.[31] On the benefits of school-to-school collaboration and federations, there is a lot that the US education system still has to learn from other countries and other sectors.

However, some promising exceptions do exist—and we can find one of them in the home of country music, Nashville, Tennessee. Despite its glitz and glamour, Nashville has more than its fair share of struggles as a city. Almost three-quarters of the students in its public school system of more than eighty thousand qualify for subsidized or free breakfast or lunch. Less than 60 percent were graduating from its twelve high schools in 2008, and they displayed consistently low performance in literacy and math.[32]

In 2009, the Nashville Area Chamber of Commerce partnered with local foundations, the mayor, and the public school system to address the need for raising achievement and for being able to recruit graduates locally for the skilled positions that awaited them in the booming medical technology and entertainment industry sectors. The chamber of commerce didn't just want students to rack up better scores in the basics; they wanted lifelong learners who would be creative and inquisitive long after they graduated. In allegiance with the public system and the city, the chamber of commerce took some bold and sometimes unfashionable decisions. It worked with schools to change the curriculum so they were no longer preparing students for trades with poor local demand, such as cosmetology. It provided externships for Nashville educators to spend in the business environments their graduates would be entering, and high-level leadership training for the educational system's leaders. It pushed and pulled the system into using data at every level to inform its decision-making process.

Some of the chamber's approaches were unexpected and even unpopular at first; for instance, its decision not to support the creation of more charter schools at the expense of Nashville's public schools. Accused by the *Wall Street Journal* of being a patsy for the teacher unions, the chamber opposed school voucher legislation in the state legislature because it didn't feel this would produce greater quality or opportunity in the city's schools. Looking back, Nashville's chamber of commerce member Marc Hill feels the chamber acted as a critical friend, exerting positive peer pressure on the district to succeed.[33]

In the midst of all its reforms to school curriculum, establishing smaller learning communities or academies within large high schools, and improving principal training, the partnership in Nashville also hired a school improvement team from England, headed by David Crossley, who came with an impressive pedigree. In England, Crossley had established a network of three hundred low-performing secondary schools that had experienced a dip in performance over at least one or two years.[34] These schools met periodically and realized they were not individual failures—but that they all struggled with a compelling and complex challenge. They were connected to higher-performing schools with similar students to theirs who helped them figure out short-term, medium-term, and long-term strategies to improve. And they had modest resources to fund their face-to-face and online interactions. The results, which one of us evaluated, had been striking: two-thirds of these three hundred schools improved at double the rate of the national average over two years.

Crossley's team worked with thirty-four high-priority schools in Nashville.[35] Their philosophy was to try to build on what the schools had, wherever possible, rather than worrying about what they lacked; to develop stronger cultures of trust and collective responsibility; to encourage and enable them to use data on an ongoing basis to guide their decisions and the interventions they made with children; and to get them to work more closely in assisting each other. One significant, federation-style change was the adoption of school-based lead principals who would guide and mentor other principals around them who needed support. This gave schools peer-to-peer assistance from within, enlarged the scope of leadership for some outstanding principals, and created new career paths allowing excellent principals to get more pay, promotion, and status by remaining close to the schools, rather than by going to work in the district office.

The results of these and other measures of schools working with schools and education working with employers have been impressive. By 2009–10, Nashville's graduation rates had exceeded 80 percent and no high schools were formally under notice of being placed in the hands of state control.

A higher shared purpose doesn't only provide uplift for its beneficiaries; it lifts its benefactors as well. We learned in chapter 1 that uplifting leadership that articulates and advances an inspiring dream can increase motivation, raise performance, and help people reach a place and a state which they might not have thought possible. The pursuit of a higher purpose through collaborations that include rivals and competitors is a counterintuitive way of achieving great social value together that organizations could never achieve alone.

Collaborative Edge

However, there is one more counterintuitive reason for collaborating with competitors that we saw in one of the most competitive cultures of all: Singapore.

Singapore's top-performing educational system is extremely competitive. Examination results at age eleven have a huge bearing on which high school children can attend. After the school day is over, many children go to receive additional private tutoring. Despite disapproval from ministers of education, this kind of educational competitiveness remains deeply ingrained in Singaporean society. At the same time, however, Sing Kong Lee, the director of Singapore's National Institute of Education that trains the entire nation's teachers, is not alone in believing that giving away your best ideas prompts you to keep inventing new ones. Education Minister Heng Swee Keat has called on schools "to form more collaborative partnerships to pursue excellence as a team, so that more schools, if not all schools, can achieve excellence."[36]

Singapore's schools are organized in self-chosen clusters of focus and interest so that schools can show what they have achieved and others can learn from their accomplishments. This applies even when these schools are still competing with each other for status and students. Back at Ngee Ann Secondary School, for example, Principal Adrian Lim described how the school had opened itself to over sixty-five schools to learn about new technology. Yet they had "never failed in competing for students" and therefore felt it had "nothing to hide." "If you are afraid of the competition," Adrian Lim told us, "you are going to be at the back end." He felt that working with another school allowed educators to "really sharpen each other" so that "both schools level up together." Yet another reason for collaborating with competitors: if you share your best ideas with your competitors, it will stimulate you to keep inventing new ones in order to stay on the leading edge of innovation.

One of the most famous parables of Christian theology is the Parable of the Talents.[37] It tells of a master with three servants who gave them all an amount of currency, in "talents," before he went away. Two of the servants invested their talents, increased their value, and were duly rewarded when their master returned. The third buried his talents, did not increase their value, and was punished as a result.

This parable struck us as deeply unfair in our youth. It seemed to reward risk and irresponsibility and punish prudence and thrift. It looked down on people like our mothers, who hung on to what precious little they had to avoid putting their family at risk.

It's not just because we're older or better off that we now see the point of the parable; it's also because we have come to appreciate that talent is a *human quality*, not just a piece of currency. It's not just something we should hope our people have and feel lucky when they do. It is something we have to discover, invest in, build, and circulate very deliberately if we are going to get great returns from it. Talent and ideas should be moved around and mobilized, not squirreled away in secret.

DuPont CEO Ellen Kullman reminds us that "science is global . . . we have to be able to move [the science] around the world very seamlessly. But the solutions [and] the applications, have to be very local."[38] Kullman's passion is to bring science to the marketplace, help customers to succeed and, in doing so, DuPont succeeds. The company changed its structure by moving decision making closer to its customers around the world; it provided more partnerships, collaboration, and solutions that are directly linked to local markets. Agriculture is a very local market that depends upon climate and prevailing conditions; therefore, a crop that thrives in one place will fail in another. To connect global science with local markets, DuPont created the *Global Collaboratory* that we mentioned in chapter 1.

It's also a personalization and integration of science and engineering. Scientists find solutions to these complex challenges at the boundaries between chemistry, biology, materials science, and engineering—so DuPont's future prosperity relies on these professionals' ability to collaborate across their specialist fields and truly integrate science with engineering. An example of this advanced cooperation took place when DuPont joined with UK-based Kilfrost to invent a deicing fluid made from bio-derived sustainable materials for Japan's All Nippon Airways. In doing so, they were first in the world to market such a product.[39]

DuPont also collaborates with its competitors in some sectors of the market such as fuels. DuPont and BP have formed a game-changing partnership to develop a fuel using biobutanol from sustainable resources. Because butanol has a higher octane than ethanol and it can be added to gasoline at 16 percent concentration, compared to the 10 percent ethanol limit, it can therefore fuel more miles per gallon. And because it has lower carbon emissions, it's also better for the environment.[40] The market is very competitive; but Kullman relishes that, "I think competition is good for the economy . . . good for us because it keeps us on our game. It keeps us focused on what's important, on how to continue to create innovation that makes a difference to our customers . . . then we, as a company, create value."[41]

So rivalries can not only be healthy; they can even be friendly—like the sporting and sibling rivalry between the Williams sisters in tennis—and if everyone takes pride and pleasure in the rising overall levels of quality, performance, and ideas that result, then people will gladly share their ideas and their talents, move them around, and find that they are rewarded as a result.

On the other hand, if you create mean-spirited environments of scarcity and fear—where you fire quotas of staff annually or set a goal to vanquish all opposition—people will bury their talents so that they won't lose them, or have them stolen. No one would want to watch Cricket Australia or any sports team if it crushed all the opposition all the time. And no one likes business monopolies that have eliminated all the viable opposition in their sector, either. This is one reason why Microsoft and other large companies have run afoul of antitrust legislation in the past. And consider the case of your local cable company. An article in the *Los Angeles Times* described the virtual monopoly that two companies—Comcast and Time Warner—hold over cable services and Internet access as "rapacious and indolent," because it discourages competition to improve services such as broadband speed and thereby disadvantages the United States in relation to international competitors.[42]

So ask yourself, and other members of your organization: what ideas are you prepared to give away, so that you might come up with new ones? This approach will not only make you collaborative, but it will also keep you on the leading edge.

Conclusion

Sometimes when we are threatened, the right response is to fight. For two years or so, Fiat Auto could just as easily have been taken over by another auto-manufacturing company, as being in charge of a partnership and then an eventual merger itself. The California Teachers' Association had to sue Governor Schwarzenegger to win back the resources that had been taken from the schools serving the state's most disadvantaged students. In fighting for something, we may have no option but to take on those who oppose us. This is the courage and the strength of uplifting leadership—but it is not without its risks. Those who oppose can be vocal, difficult, and on occasion downright threatening.

But sometimes when we stand on the city ramparts and see the enemy approaching from the distance, we can be too quick to pull up the drawbridge and bring out the cannons. We have to stop to consider that the enemy may not be the enemy at all, but an ally coming in peace or proposing a treaty or a truce. Then again, the enemy may be the enemy of your other enemy—who in that case might turn out to be your friend. For example, Nokia's merger with Microsoft is an effort to recapture its competitiveness in the smartphone market.

So before or instead of opening fire, you may choose to send out your scouts, to determine whether the people you see on the horizon are friends or foes, to gauge their intentions, learn from their ways, and explore what gains you might accomplish and what calamities you might avoid together. Sometimes we have to move toward the danger rather than attacking or avoiding it.

This chapter has identified and explored three powerful combinations of collaboration and competition:

- *Co-opetition* is the unlikely alliance between opponents who create *greater value* together than they can achieve alone.
- *Uplifting federations* that include competitors increase *social value* for the wider community as well as for each of the adversaries themselves.
- And being on the *collaborative edge* enhances *motivational value* as people push up their own performance in the comradely quest to keep on innovating and to outdo each other in a way that moves everyone up to a higher level.

Our experience and evidence of exceptional organizations makes it clear that just as collaboration and competition can no longer be neatly separated from each other, neither can the ways of combining them. There are many strategic benefits from joining together collaborative and competitive intent, from aligning joint effort, and for combining collective investment for competitive gain. Uplifting leaders know that these are the yin and yang of enduring success.

Of course, giving everything away to your opponent would be like a lamb giving itself to the fox.[43] There is a crucial difference between the wisdom of openness and the folly of unguarded innocence. But market competition need not always be a zero-sum game, in which one entity has to lose at the expense of the other. We have seen how competition with collaboration can yield enhanced learning, build a bigger and better market for all competitors, and contribute to a greater good that makes everyone feel more motivated to get out of bed and show up for work every day.

Chapter Four

Pushing and Pulling

With Kathryn Ghent

For the most part, the Commodore on the quarterdeck gets his atmosphere at second hand from the sailors on the forecastle. He thinks he breathes it first; but not so. In much the same way do the commonalty lead their leaders in many other things, at the same time that the leaders little suspect it.

—Herman Melville, Moby Dick

Pulling Together

Uplift requires the efforts of every member of the group, not just one or two. It needs a strong and committed crew. Those who don't contribute and take on collective responsibility for the uplift drag things down. Uplifting leadership entails engaging a talented team that values risk and creativity, acknowledges and tolerates honest mistakes, and has members that participate and "play" in interchangeable roles and positions. They inspire each other as leadership emerges throughout the group.

People in uplifting organizations have a deep allegiance to their colleagues, the people they serve, and a higher purpose that is greater than any individual. These organizations are able to build and sustain communities of recruitment, service to custom-ers or clients, professional practice within the organization, and support surrounding all of this.

Uplifting leadership attracts and also retains good people. Many of our organizations excelled and even turned themselves around with the support of long-standing employees who had stayed for decades. These environments generate fierce loyalty; they compel people to work hard and long to achieve what they want, and to engage others in the quest. This allegiance allows leaders to make quick and difficult decisions without losing others' support.

Allegiance in uplifting organizations is not about deference to those of higher rank. Nor is it about mutual back-scratching—that is, exchanging services in return for past favors or future rewards. Rather, loyalty or allegiance is about committing to people and caring for their lives. Uplifting leadership actively builds relationships and engenders high trust and loyalty among colleagues in order to raise expectations and take significant risks. Leaders know their people and do not impose expectations from afar. Like Alexander Dumas' three musketeers, the culture that uplifting leaders create is *one for all, all for one.*[1]

Pushing Each Other

Uplifting leadership combines the pulls of strong allegiance with powerful peer pressure. Because people are pushing themselves to outdo their previous personal best, infectious peer pressure takes hold throughout the organization and pushes *everyone* to sup-port and challenge each other. The social and emotional uplift that results elevates the organization to peak performance levels. Many leaders employ the combination of pressure and support to achieve high performance. Pressure without support creates too much stress that drags performance down; and though support without pressure may protect people from falling, it will not raise them up. The best scenario includes both elements.

In the nineteenth century, the pressure-support combination surfaced as "carrot and stick" motivation with the familiar image of a donkey enticed by a carrot at one end while being thrashed at the other. Rewards and punishments were frequently applied to factory workers required to perform boring and repetitive tasks. Management theory in the twentieth century that developed around McGregor's "Theory X" conforms to this kind of motivation, whereas his "Theory Y" assumed that individuals are intrinsically motivated to work hard.[2] What we find in uplifting leadership is the ability to pull and push people together. Uplifting organizations display a complex array of push-pull characteristics that are deeply woven into their beliefs and practices.

Commonwealth

Modern companies build loyalty through collaboration in many ways. Sometimes, their efforts are orchestrated in large symbolic events, as when Sir Stuart Rose took the unprecedented step of taking one hundred senior managers from Marks & Spencer to the cinema to watch "An Inconvenient Truth"—a documentary about Al Gore's campaign to create more awareness of the dangers attributed to global warming.[3] Sometimes, team-building efforts involve a structural reorganization such as matrix management. This involves the heads of different brands cooperating with each other on a daily basis to coordinate other functions across the whole company such as customer service. The heads of different brands at Fiat Auto, for example, have to cooperate with each other on a daily basis to coordinate other functions across the whole company such as customer service.

Sometimes, team building is embedded in an organization's habits and relationships—as in the "Dogfish Way" where everything feels "almost out of control." And sometimes, the teamwork is in the nature of the work itself. At online retailer Shoebuy.com, staff at all levels work together continuously on website innovation and redesign.[4] But teamwork and cooperation are taken to the extreme when an entire business is organized as a commonwealth.

Global sports star and style icon David Beckham's proudest moment was to deliver the Olympic Torch on the final leg of its journey to London's Olympic Park in 2012. Her Majesty the Queen had already parachuted into the stadium. Together with millions worldwide, she waited while Beckham surged along the River Thames in a high-speed Bladerunner powerboat. As he flashed under Tower Bridge with fireworks exploding into the night sky, few people realized that the unique British powerboat was fabricated from the specialized, high-end chemical products of Scott Bader Multinational.[5]

Scott Bader employs six hundred people worldwide with manufacturing sites in Europe, the Middle East, and South Africa. It makes resins and compounds for luxury yachts and high-speed Eurostar trains with a turnover of $290 million. The company is owned by its workforce and operates as a **commonwealth**—a group of people linked together by collective ownership of the business. Formed and governed by ideals of socially conscious enterprise, Scott Bader not only survives but also positively flourishes in the highly competitive technological era of twenty-first-century global capitalism.

Scott Bader was established in 1921 by a Swiss conscientious objector, Ernest Bader. For the first thirty years, it ran like any other successful business. The firm did well, making profits that gave Bader and his family financial security. At age sixty-one, Bader decided to change his company into one with a goal that so many other organizations are taking on nowadays: balancing doing well with *doing good*. He had become convinced that a world where capital employed labor was unsustainable. Labor, he felt, should own capital instead.

In 1945 Ernest Bader became a Quaker and his thoughts on industrial relations, business methods, people, and pacifism fused together. He strongly believed that collaboration was a far superior way of working and living—rather than conflict. So in 1951, he transferred the company shares to Scott Bader Commonwealth and formed an alliance with his employees by making them partners in the new company. At the same time, he pulled his workers together to agree upon a constitution for the company that included these conditions:

- A company in which all workers **functioned as partners**, not employees
- A board of directors that was **responsible to the partners**
- **Profit sharing** between partners, with a set proportion **given to charity**
- A **salary differential restricting** the highest earner to no more than seven times the salary of the lowest earner
- A commitment that **no products** made by the company would be sold or **used for making war**

Ernest Bader was a visionary who wanted the entire world to work in a way that upheld his spiritual values. His inspiring dream was to spread the wealth—while some should go to employees, some should go to good causes, including the community, social activity, and charity. Scott Bader's current managing director puts it like this:

> Ernest Bader's vision was that we shouldn't be damaging the world . . . [but rather] *helping* the world. We should be adding value . . . in everything we do, the products we make, the money we make. So there's a group called the Commonwealth that is there to manage social development and charitable giving. We give away £140,000 a year. One per cent of group salary

goes to charity. These values attract staff and create
loyalty. There is a real sense of caring for the company,
the community and the employees.

The historic sense of allegiance that Scott Bader employees
have had to their company, its purpose, and each other has been
a compelling source of attraction and retention. It has given
the company monumental pulling power, as its Learning and
Development manager recalls: "One of the reasons that attracted
me to this company was this common trust [and] ownership. I fell
in love with the ideals that Scott Bader has tried to uphold since
its inception." The director of human resources stressed how "our
key principles are trust . . . we [value] honesty. You've got to be
honest in your dealings. All of our employees should be challenging each other but doing it in a respectful way."

This is what authors John Hagel, John Seeley Brown, and
Lang Davison call *The Power of Pull*—the capacity of organizations to draw people to them through their purposes and principles, and the ability of leaders of all kinds to draw others toward
them with their passions and enthusiasms for their products, their
work, and each other.[6] The power of pull is about the importance
of pulling people in to what you are offering—as much as, or more
than, pushing ideas out to them. Traditionally, Scott Bader has
done this in a highly distinctive way, as a commonwealth.

Scott Bader is a company, a charity, and a business without
external shareholders. Its unique governance structure helps
to ensure that no single individual wields too much power at
the expense of others. The commonwealth owns the company
and is the ultimate authority. It meets quarterly as do the various
boards. The trustees have strong external representation and are
not involved in the day-to-day running of the business. Trustees
must agree to any changes to the constitution and have powers to
act in a crisis. The commonwealth board holds the shares of Scott
Bader in trust. It has six elected directors and loses two each year,
and any member can stand for election.

In post–World War II Britain, a firm built on collective owner-ship with these self-imposed restrictions was given little chance of survival—yet Scott Bader grew from strength to strength. The firm used the power of its intrinsically motivated workforce to navigate the strike-ridden decades of the 1960s and 1970s Britain far better than many of its competitors.

However, the emergence of a truly global market in the chemical industry in the late twentieth century posed more serious challenges to the company's viability. In the face of international competition and expanding markets, Scott Bader's family-like atmosphere of cooperation turned into one of increasing paternalism and collec-tive complacency. A job with Scott Bader was seen as a job for life. The workforce aged with the company. When vacancies occurred, the company promoted internally wherever possible. This lack of new blood severely limited ideas and innovation.

Although the products' quality remained high and the price was right, management and business practices became antiquated. People began to view Scott Bader as a steady but unimaginative firm. Risk taking was avoided rather than rewarded. Profit margins got slimmer and the rate of turnover steadily declined. It seemed that the company needed a bit of a push—for its own sake.

New managing director Philip Bruce arrived in 2005. In his own words, "The place was dying. It was ossifying. If Scott Bader hadn't been employee-owned, this place would probably be shut or would have been acquired by a multinational." There was a deeply embedded belief that the company's key purpose was not to make a profit but to promote its social responsibility. Bruce remembers a company meeting where someone actually said, "'Scott Bader is not here to make profits.'" "Where does the money come from?" Bruce responded. "It was a bit like the magic dust had been dropped on Scott Bader and we could get whatever we wanted. And somehow, profit wasn't important."

In 2003, the company was facing a financial crisis and by 2005 Scott Bader desperately needed an upturn in its fortunes and the uplifting leadership that could bring about this change.

The subsequent transformation of Scott Bader, in a way that has managed to remain true to the company's guiding principles, has been remarkable. The firm is once again highly successful, returning profits of $9.2 million. It was still donating to charity by 2007, and had invested profits in expansion during the world financial downturn. The company opened new plants in Croatia and the United States, operating on the same principles. Ten percent of the workforce is now dedicated to research and development. In 2012, Scott Bader was shortlisted as a finalist in the UK Private Business Award for the Technical Innovation of the Year with their industrial primer–less structural adhesives. So—how did uplifting leadership achieve all of this?

The first thing to alter the firm's course was the appointment of a new board chairman, who took over for a former chair described as "a nice man but not really that pushy with the organization."[7] This new leader had an ambitious outlook. He'd been with a major chemical multinational and was instrumental in selecting the current managing director, Philip Bruce, who was headhunted from outside the company, whereas the previous managing director had been promoted internally from head of human resources. A product manager told us,

> A change in leadership was essential if the company was to survive. It was clear that Philip coming in did actually completely revitalize the company and, yes, nearly all the executive team changed. As a result, new energy was put into the business. I think if he hadn't come in and made the changes that he's made, we wouldn't be here now.

Bruce knew that he had to slaughter a number of sacred cows in order for Scott Bader to survive. Although there was a clear move to push some staff out, this was entirely at odds with the prevailing culture. So instead of taking action immediately,

Bruce gathered some intelligent data. He initiated a customer survey that provided a quick reality check. It supplied solid evidence that they'd need to establish higher targets in order to meet clients' needs. The resulting pressure opened the way for a new performance management system that in turn provided evidence of underperformance. The whole company now realized that profits had disappeared and that some employees were just not doing their share. With the board responsible to its workforce, it took the tough decisions to dismiss the people who couldn't change.

Bruce initiated a cultural reawakening. His challenge was to uphold Scott Bader's values while moving the company back into the black. He had to balance the firm's commercial and social responsibilities. The overriding and originally admirable allegiances of Scott Bader's staff to their social causes and to each other had eventually eclipsed and then eliminated the basic concern for bottom-line profitability—and without this, there would be no company to employ its workers, serve its clients, or donate to the charities it supported. It was completely unbalanced—all pull and no push. Job security came at the expense of company earnings. Bruce described the dual nature of his incoming challenge in terms of figuring out Ernest Bader's inspiring dream: "how to organize or combine a maximum sense of freedom, happiness and human dignity in our firm without loss of profitability."

The firm's culture has gone from benevolent and paternalistic to a more realistic and beneficial outlook: **collectively responsible and accountable**. A training and development program got people to take more responsibility for their own work. Management encouraged new ideas in order to stimulate invention and placed more emphasis on research and development. Stockpiles of inventory were reduced and the supply chain was streamlined through improved use of data. These modernized working practices restored the profits that would safeguard the firm and its future for the next generation.

Although people and priorities had to change at the top, it was just as important that many of the staff below the executive level at Scott Bader remained the same. Customers experienced continuity in their relationships, and the company's distinctive values of cooperation, ethical service, and charitable giving persisted and were protected. Even after all the painful restructurings, a senior executive noted, "Our retention levels are still high. In terms of the vast majority of our customer relations, the people that dealt with you last year are probably still here. So if you're a customer phoning up again, you'll probably speak to the same person. And they will know about you. Those relationships are very, very strong."

Uplifting leadership at Scott Bader was able to combine radical change and cultural continuity in ways that restored profitability while protecting the company's unique brand of ethical integrity. Even in times of economic austerity, Scott Bader still donates the same proportion of profits to charitable causes. It draws its members together to pull and push each other to higher levels of performance. A new sense of urgency exists alongside a continuing sense of loyalty. Powerful allegiance along with positive performance leads to earned trust based on *actual accomplishment*, rather than blind trust in loyalties for their own sake. The cherished organizational past of social cooperation and ethical integrity has been reconciled with the modern business practices required for a globally competitive future. There is new thinking at the top, but a blend of continuity and renewal underneath. Everyone at the company appreciates the fact that you cannot contribute to the world and its future if you fail to preserve your own existence.

Loyalty to causes and communities is an important asset in all organizations, but *only if* it serves these higher purposes and does not become a law unto itself. Allegiances that stifle innovation, protect mediocrity, perpetuate groupthink, and promote collective self-interest over the pursuit of a greater good can lead an organization into eventual decay. But when cooperative movements are able to retain their ethical principles of equity, justice, and human association—while themselves being able to adapt and move with the economic times—cooperation strengthens competitiveness instead of weakening it. In this way, workplace communities can use the profits they protect and create to advance the ethical purposes that are important to them.

Sticking Together

One of the most important elements of common allegiance that pulls people together is teamwork. Every successful business in the twenty-first century relies on this, whether or not it's visible to its clients or customers. Teamwork is a vital ingredient in uplifting organizations—and because it's often most visible in sports, we turn to an example from the world of athletics to explore how to create effective teams.

The idea of team, team player, and team spirit in sports goes back a long time. But the word "team" actually dates back to Middle English and older Northern European languages. Here, a team was a group of animals that was yoked together—like a team of oxen. Intriguingly, in this early usage, to team meant "to draw or pull."[8]

In modern sports, teams don't mainly push, force, or drive change; rather, they draw and pull it. Teams that are tightly bound together move people upward and pull them forward toward an inspiring and important destination or goal.

One of the world's oldest team sports is hurling. Played at the speed of ice hockey by fifteen players per team, players hit, pass, or carry a stitched leather ball, called a *sliotar*, with a short wooden stick flattened at one end, called a *hurley*. The all-Ireland hurling finals draw capacity crowds of over eighty thousand to Croke Park, in Dublin, one of the largest sports stadiums in Europe nowadays.

In Ireland, hurling has always been a rallying point of national identity. It's a rough game that often turns violent, but still remains an immensely popular amateur sport for spectators and participants alike. There is a network of over twenty-five hundred clubs across Ireland. Boards for all thirty-two Irish counties organize competitions between teams in every parish and village throughout the land. The game is a powerful pulling force for local communities as well as for Irish identity.

The walls of the public bar in Langton's Hotel, Kilkenny, are lined with photographs celebrating decades of successful hurling teams that have played in their county's black and amber stripes.[9] Enjoy a pint of beer at the bar and you will soon hear stories of hurling heroes. In County Kilkenny, hurling dominates all other sports. Between 2000 and 2012, Kilkenny won nine all-Ireland senior hurling championships, the equivalent of American football's Super Bowl. These exceptional performances occurred despite the fact that Kilkenny has fewer GAA clubs than most counties in Ireland, and is in an amateur sport that prevents teams compensating for these shortfalls by signing players born outside the County.

In Kilkenny, hurling starts at an early age. To Brendan O'Sullivan, a selector for his county at minor level, "hurling is a way of life. You grow up with it from the time you're born until you die. It's in your blood. No matter which part of the county you go to, every part of it has hurling." Suffice it to say, the sport pulls lots of people in.

Ordinary people from everywhere in Kilkenny voluntarily dedicate time, effort, and money to support their local hurling team. And if Kilkenny people can give their all, Head Coach Brian Cody believes, then so too must their team. So the club has "to instill deep appreciation of the opportunity that the players have out of respect for the tradition that's in Kilkenny hurling team and Kilkenny's hurling jersey." "It's a tradition that's been there for as long as the GAA is there," Cody observes.

"The players' fathers and grandfathers have been touched by hurling all their lives. It's a huge honor and responsibility for them to pass that on to [future generations]."

Remembering where they came from, appreciating the community that supports them, and eagerly passing all this on to the next generation of players means that the team *knows* it has to pull together. When Cody was appointed at the start of the 1999 season, Kilkenny had not won the All-Ireland Championship for seven years. But as with the US women's soccer team, Cody's priority was not to regain victory. It was to *develop team spirit* throughout the organization. He wanted everyone to "work very, very hard," to be "honest" and "genuine." "We established that spirit," he said; and it became, in his view, "the cornerstone of the success" the team had beginning in 2000.

Team spirit is deliberately constructed and starts early, when children begin to play the game. Kilkenny adopts an inclusive attitude to hurling by trying to involve as many youngsters as possible in real games, stressing the importance of *enjoying the game* rather than winning. Selector Brendan O'Sullivan emphasizes the value of participation and involvement. "There are no subs. Twelve lads play," he says. "That's it . . . They're not sitting on a bench on a freezing morning hoping they might get on." Every team member is given the chance to be part of the action.

Mutual respect is an essential part of team spirit at every level. Nobody should get above himself—or anyone else, either. Senior team selector Martin Fogarty refers to "the respect everybody in the squad has for everybody else." Even the best players will say, '*if* I'm picked' and they mean it genuinely." Kilkenny players are encouraged to acknowledge everything they accomplish in hurling, but not to let it go to their heads. In Cody's words, it is essential "to stay grounded." He constantly warns players: "If you lose track of where you're coming from, what you're about, or what you're representing—and if you suddenly think you've become above your station—it doesn't lend itself to prolonged success."

Like the coaches at Burnley Football Club, Martin Fogarty is acutely aware that "if you are the top player [who starts] to get notions of yourself, it could pull the whole show down."

If team spirit depends on and calls for mutual respect and genuine humility, it also requires *honest self-appraisal* about failures as well as successes. There's a push here as well as a pull—indeed, the pull is also a kind of push. Kilkenny players are encouraged to think about their own performances, to be honest with themselves and each other, and to face up to the consequences. "There's honesty within the camp," leading player Derek Lyng observed. "If you're not going well in training, you know yourself the likelihood is you're not playing—and that's just the way it is. So you have to kind of pick yourself up, dust yourself off and get on with it."

Of course, this isn't always easy. Sometimes peer support has to turn into peer pressure. In Martin Fogarty's words, "You can shout and roar from the line if you want to, but it won't matter if the players aren't buying into it. The players demand that of each other. And if there's a new player and he's not supporting or working, the [other] lads will tell him so."

Team spirit is an inspiring and all-pervading force that pulls and draws players together and upward—a feeling of excitement, energy, and flow that infuses joy and exhilaration, bringing people to their peak. We find this kind of quality in a tight unit of highly capable and variable individuals that still acts as one body for a single cause, who will push each other forward as well as pull together.[10] Team spirit makes what players feel part of into a source of meaning, challenge, and emotional uplift that enhances the team's performance—and the community's spirits in the process.

Peer Pressure

The push-pull dynamics of corporate turnaround in the context of cooperative traditions is crucial, as are the interactive elements of pushing and pulling that compose high-performance athletic teams. But how might this concept apply to educational reform in poor urban communities—not just in "this or that" school, but in whole communities of schools in highly impoverished areas?

London's affluent West End contains some of the greatest concentrations of private wealth in the Western world. But next to the site of the 2012 Olympics along the Thames sits London's East End—home of some of the nation's poorest communities. The population grew rapidly during the 1800s as London's docks expanded to service the growing British Empire. Like New York City, the East End attracted waves of immigrants—French Huguenots, Irish, Ashkenazi Jews.[11] Starting in 1988, poor Bangladeshi immigrant refugees, fleeing from the flood disasters across the Bay of Bengal, became the most recent of these waves.

The East End contains the borough of Tower Hamlets and parts of Hackney. In terms of poverty, the East End is among the worst areas in the country. In 1996, Tower Hamlets—with forty-two thousand students in ninety-seven schools—was 149th out of 149 local authorities (school districts) in England—that is, rock bottom in the national educational achievement rankings, with Hackney next to bottom. Although the East End was once home to a thriving dockland industry, the three decades from the 1960s onwards were bleak ones for the borough. In the 1970s, the original docks were closed when shipping moved along the Thames estuary, and the old docklands area was devastated by unemployment. Those who could find work moved away, leaving empty factories and tenement blocks as icons of urban decay. There was little work for the people left behind who—it seemed initially—brought few obvious skills to their community.

Over the next twenty years, the London Docklands Development Corporation transformed much of the area into the booming new financial center housed in the glitzy glass towers of Canary Wharf. But although this created eighty-two thousand new jobs, it was mainly commuters who took them—meaning that the local population still found themselves out of work. By 2001, Tower Hamlets still had the highest unemployment rate in Britain.[12]

Generations of poverty in Tower Hamlets gave rise to degenerating expectations for children and families in the community.[13] Teachers who worked there might have felt they were "doing good in the East End"—but they didn't anticipate much in the way of results. One former school head teacher from the 1980s recalled how "the opinion of what children in Tower Hamlets could do was absolutely awful. When I went to visit the school and asked why there were no novels in the library, I was told it's because the children can't read. I asked some of the kids what they were good at in school—and they [said that they] were good at fighting and sewing." It was generally accepted by parents, teachers, and students alike that as long as the children were safe and cared for in school, nobody expected much in the way of academic achievement. No one put any pressure to push for higher standards.

How do you create uplift from such desperate beginnings? The first step is to argue strongly that children born in poverty can achieve the same high standards as anyone else, given the right support in school. This is what Christine Gilbert encouraged when she became director of education for Tower Hamlets at a time when it was the lowest performing Local Authority in the country. Gilbert already had an impressive educational pedigree when she arrived in Tower Hamlets. As a former high school principal and successful director in a high-performing London local authority she came with a proven track record of success. She also had a determined dream that children in Tower Hamlets could do as well as those in her former, more prosperous local authority, as long as they had the right support.

Gilbert instructed her school coaches and consultants to work with head teachers and set ambitious test score targets together. The Local Authority provided schools with detailed data about students' progress that schools matched with their own assessments. Head teachers predicted the likely outcomes in test scores at the end of the year based on students' prior performances. They then went back to their teachers to discuss what it would take to stretch individual pupils further with extra support—before, during, and after school. These ambitious goals required extra effort but were still realistic provided the support worked. Schools ended up with a target range between a predicted level and a more ambitious level that pushed and pulled the schools to higher performance. Working this way, schools in Tower Hamlets began setting—and meeting—highly ambitious targets.

The process of uplift was more than a technical and statistical one of target setting. It also required that members of the community raised their expectations for what they could achieve. They needed to see energy and assets where others saw only problems and disadvantage. Few people expressed this as well as Kevan Collins, the leader of Tower Hamlets in 2009 at the time of our study and Christine Gilbert's successor.

We arranged to meet Kevan in a tiny Bangladeshi restaurant just off Tower Hamlet's bustling thoroughfare, Brick Lane. As we took our seats beneath a TV showing Bollywood music videos, Kevan could barely suppress his excitement about his work.

Kevan Collins hasn't just led Tower Hamlets. He is one of its proud residents and, as such, wanted to take us on a walk through his neighborhood. He showed us the alleyways where Jack the Ripper committed his gruesome murders.[14] Then he pointed to the brass foundry where the American Liberty Bell was forged. Around the corner was one of the most remarkable symbols of the borough's vibrant, diverse history and identity—a tiny synagogue tucked into a corner of London's largest mosque. And then he gestured with visible pride toward the people all around us—first- and second-generation Bangladeshis, running small local businesses, hustling on their cell phones, bringing their energy to the streets. "I think the Bengali community is very confident about itself," he said. "There's a confidence and verve about: 'We can do things' and that's important."

During difficult times, one of the tasks of uplifting leadership is to connect people to earlier periods and identities that bestowed a sense of pride and to connect these to more hopeful possibilities that lay ahead. Both Collins and Christine Gilbert understood this. Tower Hamlets, Gilbert said, was "a very seductive area (that) just gets hold of you." A secondary school head teacher said "there is something sexy about the East End. There's lots of history. And if you're working for one of those big city firms, you can say: 'We're working with a school in the East End.' It's got quite a cachet to it."

Reconnecting people to this history enriches their commitment to the borough's new narrative of aspiration and togetherness. It also inspired Gilbert and Collins to take a stand against the borough's appalling educational record, the educators' low expectations, and using poverty to explain away school failure. It combined the pull of identity and community with the push of ambitious targets and unyielding expectations.

Over ten years, the uplifting leadership throughout the borough brought Tower Hamlets from being the worst performing district in England to a place in the top half of the country. One way the schools achieved this themselves was by working or pulling together. One former head teacher pointed to the "very strong collegiate approach among the heads. . . There's a lot of support for each other," she said. "However daunting [any challenge] was, there'd always be somebody else that you could call [on for feedback and support].'" When one of the borough's thirteen secondary schools fell into failure, all the other twelve schools rallied round to help it.

But even though they collaborated, Tower Hamlet's secondary schools still retained a competitive edge. Christine Gilbert explained that "once the school up the road is doing better than you, [you might] say you're not competitive—but you absolutely are. You're looking at what that school did, and how, and why." She went on, "The secondary heads always collaborated well, but actually, underneath it, they were competing, too."

The unspoken, underlying message that provides that push is: "If they can do it, why can't we?" There is competitiveness here, to be sure; but it is not born of a desire to outdo everyone else merely to show that you're better than they are. It is more about competing with *yourself* to be as good as you can. Because the system is so highly collaborative, a school that does better than the rest willingly shares its secrets of success to benefit students throughout the community. This is the essence of uplifting leadership: schools pull together and share their best ideas, while simultaneously employing peer pressure to achieve more for the sake of all students.

Achievement in a variety of industries is enhanced when the strong help the weak. This usually serves to raise the standard for everyone by promoting improvement throughout the market or industry. It's not all about saintly self-sacrifice; friendly rivalry plays its part as well.

Too much of the modern reform agenda in public education is all push and no pull. It pushes people out if they can't deal with the job or lift up the scores. And it tries to push teachers up by offering them performance bonuses if they show they can get results.[15] When Mayor Michael Bloomberg imposed his corporate model of merit pay on the New York City public school system, it cost the Department of Education $20 million in bonuses. But the model and the money had no impact on student performance or teachers' attitudes.[16] But Tower Hamlets' educators set ambitious targets together. They respect and expect a lot from their students and their community. And they pull and push each other forward in a spirit of undying mutual support and healthy, friendly competition.

Conclusion

We've seen how some corporate leaders believe that leadership should foment fear by replacing 10 percent or more of management every year and making everyone compete for their jobs.

But we've also seen evidence of how working in high performing teams is a more effective approach. It pulls people together through engagement and trust, and encourages these motivated team members to push each other better and harder than superiors can push them from above. A key study of peak performing organizations in sports by Clive Gilson and his colleagues attributes much of the success of these performers to the strength and operation of their teams off the field as well as on it.[17] Gilson and his colleagues conclude from their study, "[Feeling] safe in our relationships . . . and at one with our inner selves . . . enables mental clarity, which is essential for focus and peak performance."[18]

Scott Bader combined an ingrained ethic of cooperation with the commitment to profit making that was as strong as the company's world-class resins. At Kilkenny hurling, the culture spread through the volunteers and into the deliberate cultivation of team spirit. Tower Hamlets' educators practiced uplifting leadership by sharing success and supporting each other while at the same time exerting peer pressure to push up standards.

The results of combining pushing and pulling, and treating *pulling as pushing*, are unmistakably beneficial. Kilkenny has been the highest performer in its sport and an inspiration for the community. Tower Hamlets refused to accept poverty as an excuse for low educational outcomes and turned the worst school results in England into achievements that topped the national average. And Scott Bader has returned from the edge of ruin to combine the virtuous principles of cooperation, co-ownership, and social contribution with luxury products that have an Olympian sense of style. But none of this success is a result of hunch or intuition. Rather, it is based on reliable and meaningful data, which we explore more deeply in the next chapter.

Chapter Five

Measuring with Meaning

With Alex Gurn

I personally measure success in terms of the contributions an individual makes to his or her fellow human beings.

—Margaret Mead

Data World

One inescapable fact of the twenty-first century is the permeating presence of *data*. Whether it's the bar codes on our shopping preferences, the calorie-counting apps on our smartphones, or the facial recognition software that can help track down terrorists, data devices are all around us, affecting more and more of our choices and decisions. What distinguishes uplifting organizations and their leaders is not the fact that they are data-driven, but how they *define and draw on* the data that are important to them.

Uplifting organizations carefully and systematically mark, monitor, and manage their progress toward success. They don't just know where they are going and how to get there. They also review their progress to see how far they have come, determine how well they are doing, and gauge whether they're staying on course. They use a range of progress indicators and performance goals—personally meaningful, broadly shared, and demonstrably fair measures of what leaders and followers are collectively trying to achieve. Uplifting leaders don't merely depend on inspiration and imagination. They also know how crucial it is to intelligently use performance data to move everyone forward and upward in ways that are

- *Meaningful* and valid to the people who use them
- *Connected* to the organization's core purposes and processes
- *Balanced* rather than lopsided in their emphasis
- *Timely* in their application and accessibility
- *Integrated* with professional judgment, instead of overriding it
- Embedded in valued *relationships*; not imposed from on high or afar

Members of uplifting organizations aren't blindly driven by data, or plunged into panic by the threat of imposed, short-term performance targets. Their metrics are meaningful, their targets are owned, and they use data to strengthen rather than undermine employee judgments.

There are many upsides to how people use data, and more than a few dark or just plain daft sides as well. Both aspects are evident in all three sectors that we explore in this book. Let's start by going to the dark side.

Dark Data

Thanks to Michael Lewis's best-selling book *Moneyball*—which was also made into a movie starring Brad Pitt—the role of performance metrics in improving the results of professional sports teams is now very well known and appreciated. *Moneyball* is a gripping account of how systematic and detailed use of player performance statistics raised the performance of the underfunded Oakland Athletics (also called the Oakland A's) baseball team to World Series standard.[1]

In 2002, Oakland's new general manager Billy Beane brought in a Harvard economics graduate to use performance statistics as a basis for selecting new players—a system he called "performance scouting." This selection process had previously been based on the coaches' experience and intuition. Beane most favored the statistic that best predicts the performance of a team over a season: on-base percentage, or the proportion of times a batter is able to reach base without getting out. There are both dramatic and unimpressive ways of doing this; but Beane determined that how a batter gets onto first base is immaterial. All that mattered was the performance and the result—even if it looked ugly.

Oakland played the percentages with remarkable results. More players made it to first base—which of course got them one step closer to home plate and scoring. Year after year, Oakland got to the playoffs to face teams who made triple their salaries. For the Oakland A's, cumulative evidence defied individual coaches' experience, intuition, and habit. Data were more important than experience. Stats trumped judgment. The use of performance stats that Oakland pioneered in America is now standard throughout professional baseball and other sports. And it is spreading to other sectors as well.

Bill Gates is a convert to metrics, not just someone who has a geeky interest in making analogies to baseball stats—although he has certainly done that too. Gates wrote in the *Wall Street Journal* at the start of 2013 how, over the previous year, he had become struck by how measurement could contribute to improving the human condition. One of the examples he picked out was the progress Ethiopia was making in reaching one of the United Nations' ten Millennium Goals that it set in 2000—reducing infant mortality by two-thirds by 2015.[2]

Inspired by the Indian state of Kerala, which the data showed had achieved success in reducing infant mortality by establishing a network of community health care posts, Ethiopia set up fifteen thousand of its own posts across the country. The centers are now able to track children's births and deaths and to monitor more carefully where vaccines or mosquito nets have or have not been provided. Measurement and tracking isn't the only part of Ethiopia's strategy, of course; but Gates believes it has played a significant part in reducing infant mortality by 60 percent since 1990, and will contribute to the country achieving this significant Millennium Goal by 2015.

This is a thoughtful and hopeful approach from Gates—definitely better than fly-by philanthropy that just awards grants and eventually gets a report at the end, or philanthropic investment that has to wait years before it sees any measurable returns. But as inspired as Gates and many others have become by data-driven improvement in sports, philanthropy, and business, the outcomes are not always so positive or benign.

In their book *Judgment on the Front Line: How Smart Companies Win by Trusting Their People*, Chris DeRose and Noel Tichy describe their consultancy relationship with a supermarket chain.[3] One thing that they found as they tried to help the chain improve its performance was that the company had started to use scanning metrics to set targets, in terms of the numbers of shoppers that checkout staff processed per hour. Under this new and inescapable pressure, staff started to avoid any time-consuming personal interactions that might prevent them from reaching the target, such as helping older customers or even *making eye contact* with shoppers. Target-driven monitoring had a negative impact on the human relationships with customers—the very things on which the supermarket ultimately depended. This, say DeRose and Tichy, is just one example of how businesses can overuse metrics to standardize performance in ways that undermine the judgments of frontline workers.

In any organization where data turn into an overriding obsession in an atmosphere of top-down control and poor relationships, the result is usually dangerous or just plain daft. To understand how this works, let's return to sports—not to the media magic of *Moneyball*, but to the place where the use of data to drive improvements in player performance first began. This takes us back behind the Iron Curtain, to the days of the Cold War.

The first known exponent of systematic use of performance data in sports was Valeri Lobanovsky, coach for the former Soviet Union's Dynamo Kiev soccer team from the mid-1970s to the early 1990s. Four decades ago, Lobanovsky decided to apply the principles of scientific Marxism to soccer management. Standing by the pitch with a notebook and pencil, he noted the different moves that individual players made and connected these to team performance outcomes. When Lobanovsky purchased a large computer—arousing the suspicions of the KGB in the process—his goal was to combine science and technology to create the perfect soccer team.

In *How Soccer Changed the World*, author Franklin Foer describes how Lobanovsky applied numerical values to every successful and unsuccessful action in the game.[4] He put the data through the computer to produce calculations of "intensivity, activity, error rate," and so on. Lobanovsky was seeking a perfect system that his players could adopt almost automatically. He even organized five-a-side matches where players had to play blindfolded. According to Foer, Lobanovsky's system

> rewards a very specific style of play: **physical and frenetic**. Players work tirelessly to compile points. They play defense more aggressively than offense, because that's where points can be racked up. Lobanovsky's system mimicked the Soviet regime under which it was conceived. Like the Soviets, it stifles individual

initiative. Nothing in Lobanovsky's point valuation measures creativity or daring. A vertical pass receives the same grade as a horizontal pass; a spectacular fake means nothing.

Lobanovsky created charts depicting numerical targets that his players had to meet for things like tackles, shots on goal, or headers on goal, depending on the overall team tactics.[5] "All life is a number," Lobanovsky once said.[6]

Though this data-driven system produced consistently high performance within the Soviet league, it also created *inflexibility* among the players. When overseas players from Africa and elsewhere came to play in the Ukraine in later years, they discovered that their artistic and creative style could not fit into the system. In large part, their struggles stemmed from the fact that they had no identity outside the team.

These days, almost all professional athletic teams use data as a matter of course. Leading soccer clubs place video cameras around the pitch, send the recorded movies away so that metrics can be compiled for individual and team performance factors, and then have in-house performance analysts examine these. There is a wider range of data now. But how do the teams use this data? What sense do people make of the numbers that the computers crunch out?

One of Burnley Football Club's former performance analysts described how, in one World Cup soccer competition, teams combined video evidence with the practice of placing microchips in players' boots to gather additional data about the number of steps they took during a game. Some coaches then started to pressure players to use more energy during games, even setting "step targets." Burnley's analyst described how "some players started doing extra steps when the ball went out of play (out of sight of the cameras) to up their stats." The players would then be able to tell their manager, "Yes, I've done my job this week." When data are used in this way—insensitively, in high-threat situations—this kind of perverse outcome can easily result. People can end up taking lots of extra unnecessary steps just to comply with the required target.

Most readers will have seen the same kinds of effects in business. It's called "gaming the system"—a process that engages people's creativity in taking extra little steps to undermine and circumvent the system when it's trying to catch them out, rather than in supporting the system to achieve its goals. Companies can insist that their employees sign in and sign out, only to find that people are having friends do the signing in for them. They can distribute approval and rewards to people whose cars are the last to leave the parking lot; but then people just start to leave their cars in the lot overnight. The immense effort that companies like Enron put into "creative accounting" simply leads to exaggerated performance outcomes and fabricated results. During the international banking crisis of 2007, huge corporations committed outright fraud by using statistical manipulation to yield short-term profits or to manufacture the appearance of them.[7]

None of these kinds of extra steps get you any closer to achieving core purposes—and the point applies to public services too. When the UK government imposed an intensive culture of targets to try to improve the efficiency of public services, newsrooms became flooded with bizarre tales of the extra steps public employees were taking in order to "deliver" on those targets. Police officers reduced crime rates by spending most of their time on types of crime that were easier to solve and by redefining some hard-to-solve crimes as misdemeanors.[8] Hospital staff met their targets for reduced patient waiting times in the emergency room by having ambulances drive the sick and injured around the block until the ER could process them within the targeted time.[9] Contracted rail repair workers imperiled passenger safety by mending broken rails within targeted time periods, but they neglected the undergirding ballast and supporting ties that could not be fixed within those periods.[10]

In public education systems that are driven by relentless demands to increase test scores within very short timescales, the behaviors that result are equally problematic. In 2009, 35 educators in Atlanta, Georgia, were indicted for cheating. An investigation had initially detected "statistically improbable increases" across the district and further investigation revealed widespread cheating among 178 educators in 44 schools.[11] The district's former superintendent, previously a winner of a national award for raising achievement scores in her district, was charged with theft, because the test score increases were linked to bonuses in her pay.

Critics were concerned about the fact that all the indicted educators were black. Atlanta's cheating scandal, they said, was the tip of a much bigger iceberg. George W. Bush's No Child Left Behind Legislation of 1996 required schools to make "Adequate Yearly Progress" (AYP), not just on average, but for every significant subcategory of students such as those with special needs or who did not speak English as their first language.[12] All US schools had to achieve levels of proficiency in English and mathematics for all subcategories of students by 2014. If they failed to meet their targets, an escalating series of punitive interventions occurred. These ultimately included firing the principal, closing the school, or replacing it with a charter school.

This reform strategy—evaluating schools by whether they reached imposed targets in student test scores and then applying sanctions to those that fell short—was an extreme version of what England and other countries were already using.[13] The very existence of the schools and the educators' jobs came to depend on continuous increases in scores on one or two tests. Thus, because their survival depended on it, some educators introduced a range of cynical, unethical, and eventually corrupt practices to meet their targets and avoid punitive sanctions—including these:

- Spending more time on test preparation than actually teaching students.
- Excluding students who had little chance of passing from test taking, or "encouraging" them to transfer to other schools.
- Narrowing the curriculum to just those subjects that were tested, and thereby excluding learning in areas such as the arts, physical education, and creativity.
- Lowering standards on statewide tests so that passing became easier.
- Concentrating excessive attention on students who were scoring just below the passing threshold—to get quick returns with just a bit more effort on their upcoming test results.
- Blatant cheating by altering students' test papers after they had finished, or by displaying answers on the classroom wall.

Testing students is important, of course; how else would teachers know what their students have learned so that they can plan their next lessons? But *relentlessly testing* students at the expense of teaching them, in order to put pressure on teachers, is unfair for both groups. Beyond the disturbing instances of outright cheating in Atlanta and elsewhere, there is a culture of punitive accountability in education that rates and ranks schools on single measures of crudely assessed achievement. Test scores reduced to a single number simply do not and cannot capture the range of what students are able to achieve. It is like saying that if you have one foot in a bucket of steam and another in a bucket of ice, on average, you should be comfortable! More importantly, these very simple kinds of testing processes tend to take place at the end of the school year when it is too late for educators to apply anything they've learned from the results. It doesn't give teachers the kinds of data that can help improve their current students' performance. Once accountability strategies concentrate on only one or two aspects of performance and use blunt tools to assess it, the whole system is distorted to deliver these results, even at the cost of its core purposes.

This perverse process is known as Campbell's Law, named after Dartmouth College professor Donald T. Campbell, who stated that

> The more any quantitative social indicator is used for social decision-making, the more subject it will be to corruption pressures and the more apt it will be to distort and corrupt the social processes it is intended to monitor.[14]

Sometimes, performance targets inflict even worse consequences than going to jail for cheating on your tests, falling into financial ruin, or taking lots of time-wasting steps that just aren't necessary. They become matters of life and death.

The fate of the Titanic was sealed not just by an iceberg it couldn't avoid but also by a timed target for crossing the Atlantic that its captain wouldn't abandon, even when, in bad weather, it was a clear threat to basic passenger safety. In the mountain climbing community, the drive to reach the summit the closer it gets, even though doing so carries extremely high risks of dying in the attempt when the weather closes in, or supplies have run out, is known as "summit fever."

Sometimes organizations and teams are also gripped by "summit fever" as they get closer and closer to their desired objective and start to lose sight of their core purpose and focus—with devastating results.[15]

In their controversial paper *Goals Gone Wild*, a group of Harvard Business School writers describe how, in the 1960s, the Ford Motor Company accelerated production schedules to produce a new, small car that would compete with overseas rivals.[16] The unrealistic production targets led employees to bypass safety checks—including one to the Ford Pinto's fuel tank. Explosions of this fuel tank due to faulty design led to fifty-three deaths and many injuries. The authors draw the chilling conclusion that "the specific, challenging goals (speed to market, fuel efficiency, and cost) were met at the expense of other important features that were not specified—safety, ethical behavior, and company reputation." They conclude that goals go wild when goals and targets are, among other things:

- Too *narrow*, which leads to neglect of other important aspects of performance
- Too *short-term*, which leads to neglect of longer term aspects of performance compared to metrics like quarterly returns
- Too *unrealistic*, which leads to taking unacceptable risks and engaging in unethical behavior

Overemphasizing single, short-term targets and metrics like quarterly returns or customer-processing rates can also eliminate opportunities for feedback when things go wrong—thereby leading employees to make poor decisions. For instance, shareholders might panic after one disappointing quarter, fearing that this will herald a precipitous decline. Yet a quarterly dip could just be a statistical anomaly, an unusual season in the sector, a reflection of a wider sector trend, or a temporary disruption resulting from a change in work practices. Misreading short-term blips as long-term dips can create what Yossi Sheffi calls the *bullwhip effect*: leaders overreact to a temporary shortfall in performance or demand by unnecessarily firing leaders, switching suppliers, escalating targets, selling off assets, or closing down entire sections of the operation.[17]

So it's important to be clear about the "dark side" of data. For all the faith that executives and philanthropists have in "Big Data," it can easily become "Big Bad Data" in the wrong form and in the wrong hands. This happens when the data are too blunt or narrow; when they arrive too late to be helpful; or when they are designed to buttress a few people's power and control. It happens, in other words, when people don't trust the numbers or the people using them.

Data Minding

Instead of merely *mining* all the data we can gather, we should be *minding* data with diligence and care so that they help rather than harm the people they are meant to serve. For example, using performance data in highly successful businesses does not rely solely on assessing quarterly returns. A growing number of businesses now emphasize many kinds of outcomes above the bottom line in more "balanced scorecards" of performance.[18] They don't just use metrics to assess performance, but also to stimulate collective discussion and responsibility about *how* best to improve it.

This meaningful use of measurement is especially enlightening in some parts of the Internet-based retail sector, because so many interactions that take place here are virtual rather than personal. It's also a place where product inventory doesn't really exist in the traditional sense.

In the middle of the dot-com boom of the 1990s, New England Entrepreneur of the Year Scott Savitz and banking industry colleague Craig Starble spoke about an idea of selling footware online.[19] Mike Sorabella, who later became employed with Shoebuy and was a banking colleague of theirs, recalls Craig speaking at a morning meeting at the bank during the dot-com heyday and saying "We've got to get into this dot-com business." According to Sorabella, "Craig actually threw the idea to the room that we should be selling shoes online and we all chuckled and said, 'But what should we really do?'" Savitz initially laughed off the idea. "Like many others, I did not like the concept of buying footware over the Internet," he recalled. "But the more I learned how we could make it very scalable by creating this virtual model where we teamed up directly with the manufacturers, the more I liked it."

At the time of our study in 2009, Shoebuy.com was one of the Internet's top ten most-visited apparel and accessory shopping sites—as well as one of the top ten "stickiest" websites in the

Internet shopping sector, with over a fifteen-minute average visit time among its online customers. When shoppers reach the website, they tend to stay and keep coming back. Repeat buying grew from nearly one-fifth of revenues in 2000, to more than a third in 2004, and nearly two-thirds in 2009. In 2011, Shoebuy realized a healthy profit margin per customer. The company achieved eight straight years of double-digit percentage increases in revenue growth in the first decade of this century.

Shoebuy also has very high rates of staff retention. For example, approximately 80 percent of its 2009 management team included people who had originally been hired for those roles almost a decade earlier. Shoebuy also had a strong track record of promoting entry-level staff to positions of leadership. Even in the midst of the global financial collapse in 2009—when Shoebuy's major competitor, Zappos, was forced to cut at least 8 percent of its staff—Shoebuy continued to hire employees. It thrived when competitors were struggling just to survive. From the time Savitz sold his company in 2006, until he left the company in 2011, Shoebuy continued significant revenue growth and grew bottom line faster than top line. How did the company survive the dot-com bust and then the global economic collapse when many of its competitors had to cut back or had failed altogether?

A big part of the answer lies in Shoebuy's metrics and its organizational design. It has designed and built a complex technological infrastructure and online architecture. This supports an innovative, nimble, and customer-responsive design that is high on service and low on inventory and other overhead costs. Shoebuy primarily employs a model known as *drop shipment*. Customer orders are placed and mailed directly from manufacturers' warehouses to the consumers. If you decide to send shoes back, you mail them to Shoebuy's warehouse, which also handles product returns and international shipments. The company's website serves as a portal that virtually inventories a cross-section of products in shoes, bags, accessories, and clothing from more than 1,250 manufacturing partners, connecting them with potential online consumers. Shoebuy's model avoids large backups of inventory. It is not vulnerable to fickle shifts of consumer taste and preference in footwear fashion; indeed, it capitalizes on them. As Chief Marketing Officer Jim Keller explained:

> It's important to us to make sure that we're growing the business in a healthy way—that everything we do is scalable. [We'll only] release a new program or roll out a new feature on the site in a way that we believe will scale with the business. If it's a partnership that requires somebody to hand-touch every order, it's not going to scale. You can't be selling tens of millions of pairs of shoes if somebody's got to touch every single one of them. Things need to be automated.

One aspect of scalability involves time and patience to build and test initiatives, before launching at full scale. This is made possible through Shoebuy's Web-based infrastructure and data-driven processes. Scott Savitz told us how he was "metric obsessed." Indeed, the new business he established after eventually leaving Shoebuy called Data Point Capital focuses on businesses that can leverage and scale online based on fundamentally sound metrics. Savitz loves numbers and how they can be used to inform and improve business practices. At Shoebuy, they permit complex analyses of users' interactions with the website and enable real-time responses to these engagements to be made. Every person who accesses Shoebuy.com becomes a participant in a self-study of its effectiveness. And with millions of unique website visitors each month, this translates into mountains of useful and usable data.

Shoebuy's product inventory is analyzed using an array of criteria including click-through, sell-through, margin, rate of return, repeat sales, customer surveys, and website feedback. Shoebuy's systems also analyze other information, such as how people move through the website and when they navigate away from it. One mode of inquiry is A/B testing, an approach in which one set of customers views a certain website configuration, while another set views a slightly different configuration. For instance, Shoebuy may measure whether "Add to Cart" or "Click Here to Check Out" leads to a better click-through rate. Savitz explained that things like "different titles for an email campaign and changes to the navigation bar allow for improved sales, improved repeat buying, and lifetime value."

Real-time data lead to improved design—such as offering increased and improved views inside a bag or a purse. These adjustments are continuous and nimble, yet *sustainable*. In this way, Shoebuy is able to gradually improve the site's look and feel without shocking loyal fans with sudden, massive changes in design. As a result, customers stay longer and longer on the site—giving Shoebuy its high rate of "stickiness."

Shoebuy continually seeks ways to know customers better through triangulated sets of data, but it doesn't rely on digital data alone. Shoebuy lists its phone number prominently on all Web pages and encourages customer feedback via Facebook and Twitter. It has never outsourced its customer-service functions. When Shoebuy receives an e-mail inquiry from a customer, the customer will get a human (not computer-generated) response. They strive to answer customer calls very quickly to limit hold times—and the company's executives don't hesitate to call customers personally when there is a problem. Technical data have supported customer relationships, rather than replacing them. Hard data doesn't replace "soft skills and processes"; rather, they complement each other.

Within the company itself, intelligent use of performance data guides people's decisions and actions and motivates a sense of ownership of their work. Savitz explained, "We try to enable everybody to understand what their objectives are in each of their own individual areas of business." Although Shoebuy leaders were explicit about staff expectations and benchmarks for successful performance, they also provided tools for staff to use themselves so they could exercise professional discretion and make their own judgments on the front line.

With this evidence-informed approach, Shoebuy staff regularly identify when something is not working or needs tweaking. According to Savitz, they don't hesitate to "come to us [and say] I'm having trouble here." He believes that "a lot of companies make the mistake of saying they don't want people individually to be that empowered." Yet at Shoebuy, employees are encouraged to take risks. The founders know that real-time monitoring permits swift interventions to correct errors and avert catastrophes. This enhances innovation and continuous improvement, increases employee satisfaction, and is one of the key reasons for Shoebuy's strong, award-winning record of staff retention. According to current CEO Mike Sorabella, "The culture is one where everyone is dedicated, works hard, enjoys being part of our small company and feels that they can make a difference."

Scott Savitz and his partners at Shoebuy faced doubt and even ridicule when they started up their business in a makeshift sixty-square-meter office inside a converted funeral parlor. But their bold yet sustainable business model—in which data play a central and critical role—broke the boundaries of footwear marketing and dot-com practice. Now they occupy prime corner-office space in downtown Boston.

In high-performing businesses—especially those that are knowledge- and information-based—performance measures and other data metrics are meaningful, broad, balanced, and fair. They are also timely and accessible enough to encourage innovation and risk taking yet head off large-scale errors. Instant information and intervention underpin disciplined innovation. Targets are ambitious but achievable. Performance is evaluated over longer-term as well as short-term time periods. Employees are very often involved in defining targets together. Ethics and integrity are high priorities, along with the quality of customers' experience. All of this supports rather than distracts people from their core mission and purpose. Data don't just push people harder and higher to the point of "summit fever." Instead, data lift them up, drawing them toward a vision they truly share and collectively value, with metrics that are sensible to them and help them make better judgments.

Testing Times

Data may be accepted and commonplace in business and sports, but in public education, numbers, tests, and rankings provoke intense controversy between several factions. While politicians and the business lobby tend to believe that student test score data are the key to accountability, education professionals argue that too much testing distorts the work of teaching and ultimately harms children. And there is a lot of evidence to provide the critics with ammunition in all the highly publicized examples of cheating and "gaming the system" that we described earlier.

So how can we prevent the law of perverse incentives from distorting the way that public education uses measurement and metrics? We find one potential answer in Finland, a country that, as we saw earlier, consistently performs at the top on the international PISA tests of student achievement.[20] Here, the answer is to not use test score data at all. The point is to know and teach your students well.[21]

What Finns value most in education is having highly qualified expert teachers who get to know their students by developing strong relationships with them. They're able to do this because they've been being trained rigorously in the cognitive science of how young people's brains work. Primary school teachers in Finland often teach the same class of students over several years. They have more time in the school day than teachers in any other country to plan for their students and to meet with their colleagues to discuss their students' needs. Finland does use achievement tests confidentially, with samples of students, to monitor how the system is doing overall. However, educators here understand that it is not statistically necessary to test a census of all students in order to check how the system is doing. As Finland's greatest education ambassador Pasi Sahlberg puts it, you don't need to remove all the blood from someone's body to test it. You just take a sample.[22]

The lesson we can take from Finland is not that testing is unnecessary and all you need is strong knowledge of your children and good relationships with them. Some other countries have also chosen not to use standardized testing—but with fewer well-qualified teachers, they get less impressive results. The lesson, therefore, is that the point of statistical and other kinds of data is to strengthen these professional relationships by providing additional information, establishing a clear focus, or giving feedback about impact and progress. One way to do this is for teachers to look at a wider range of data—such as teacher-designed tests that can diagnose difficulties with things like particular reading skills, classroom observations, and samples of students' work. This can enable teachers to discover, in real time, why particular students or groups of students are falling behind. Good school leaders collect and value many kinds of data to enrich the understanding that teachers have of their students and to guide the just-in-time interventions that can help them.[23]

We have seen examples of this approach in our work with ten school districts—almost one-seventh of the school districts in the province of Ontario in Canada.[24] Like Singapore and Finland, Ontario is one of four provinces that have very high scores on the international PISA measurements of student achievement. Since 2003, the province has had a highly targeted reform strategy whose goal is to raise the bar of achievement and narrow achievement gaps between students from more and less advantaged homes in literacy and mathematics in grades 3 and 6. In literacy especially, where its strategies have been most intensive, the system has made strong progress and by 2012 met a provincial target of 75 percent of students reaching proficiency (Level 3) on this test from a baseline of 58 percent in 2003.[25]

Instead of threatening underperforming schools or posting their failures on lists of shame, Ontario chose to make financial investment in them by coaching and mentoring their teachers in improved classroom practices. They offered networks of assistance that enabled struggling schools to get help from similar schools that were doing better.

Although Campbell's Law of perverse incentives still reared its head from time to time, this more supportive environment lent itself to schools that used data to deepen teachers' understanding of students' learning. One elementary school, for example, achieved steady gains in literacy results not by concentrating on borderline students or teaching to the test, but by using data to focus care and attention on all *individual children who needed it*. In this school, all the teachers cared about all the students' learning, not just those in their own class or grade. "It used to be *my* students," they said. "Now, it's *our* students." Teachers looked at how each child was progressing by consulting a "wall of data" that tracked their progress in real time in red, amber, and green. They also consulted many other kinds of evidence about students in addition to what was posted on the wall, including portfolios of their classroom work. Everyone's energy was relentlessly focused on moving these students along and lifting them up, one at a time, every week. In the words of one district staff member, "We meet them where they are and move them forward."

Schools with uplifting leadership like this have respected teachers, high levels of trust, rich and wide-ranging data, evidence that's available in real time so that prompt interventions can be made, and a strong sense of collective responsibility. In these cases, data-informed processes can and do combine with teachers' judgments about the children they know well, to improve teaching and learning.

The challenge at the moment is that elsewhere, too many educational testing practices and data-driven improvement processes are the *opposite* of what works best in business and sports. They comprise a narrow range of test-score measures that are imposed in a high-threat culture, with little or no professional involvement, and are administered too late in the year to be of any use to the students who have taken them. This provokes perverse, cynical, and even corrupt responses that undermine the fundamental purposes of what schools are supposed to do for our children and our nations. Though all this was meant to align public education with business practices of accountability, it actually does not reflect how data are used in the most successful corporations.

Conclusion

Moneyball isn't all about blindly using the numbers to drive up performance. Burnley's performance analyst and his soccer club used statistical evidence in a far more interactive and inclusive way than the Oakland A's did, and definitely more mindfully than in the scientific Marxism of Lobanovsky's soccer team at Dynamo Kiev. Burnley's analyst shared data with the coach, suggested what it meant in terms of performance or energy levels, invited players to see how their statistics compared to average performance levels in the league, and then discussed specific ways to improve together. "The data *contribute* rather than *dictate* what they should do," he commented. "Whether it is technical or tactical, you can have a different interpretation of it." Responding to the data with threats or commands would be sure to fail, he said, because to "prescribe what to do" would "take away the spontaneity and creativity" that accorded with the club's and team's philosophy of "freedom of expression." As the analyst told us, "My strength is to find that information and bring it to (the coach's) attention. From that, they can make their decisions." He went on, "I wouldn't want to start telling people what to do. I [just] want to help [the players] improve, and play their best."

Smart coaches and smart leaders of all kinds know that data don't *automatically* drive improvement in successful performance. Evidence thoughtfully informs it by combining it with judgment. In the aftermath of *Moneyball*, this truth about the complementary power of judgment and intuition is even being accepted in baseball once again.

In their book *Big Data*, authors Viktor Mayer-Schonberger and Kenneth Cukier describe many of the ways that data enter into our lives.[26] Big data, they say, are about "the ability of society to harness information in novel ways to produce useful insights or goods and services of significant value." They explain how the growing capacity to analyze vast volumes of data has made it possible to predict the spread of flu pandemics, to pinpoint the buildings most likely to be overcrowded fire hazards, and to use complex algorithms to provide just-in-time feedback in response to people's progress in their online learning.

This chapter has outlined what Big Data can do in high-performing organizations and systems. It's shown how data can make it more possible for people to reach their goals. Data helped Fiat Auto in its quest to reduce waste to zero and enabled Shoebuy.com to continuously innovate in its website designs. In education, data dashboards are making it increasingly possible to diagnose quickly and exactly where students might be struggling in their learning, and enabling teachers to take collective responsibility for all students' success. Even the California Teachers' Association that disapproves of excessive testing uses the State's Academic Performance Index to measure its progress and communicate the success of its strategy.

But after their extensive advocacy for Big Data, Mayer-Schonberger and Cukier then urge their readers to avoid turning to data for answers to *all* their problems. They point to "the special need to carve out a place for the human: to reserve space for intuition, common sense and serendipity. . . What is greatest about human beings," they say, "is what is precisely what the algorithms and silicon chips *don't* reveal."[27] Uplifting leaders attend to the human side as well as the technical side of change. In the end, it is not the replacement of human meaning and judgment by computer metrics that uplifts performance. There is no algorithm for expertise; wisdom does not manifest itself on a spreadsheet. What ultimately matters the most is how metrics are used to improve human judgment and human experience.

In the 1970s, Southland Corporation pioneered the concept of the convenience store now known as the 7-Eleven in Japan. Toshifumi Suzuki, the first CEO, placed responsibility for ordering in the hands of the store's 200,000 employees who were mostly part-time sales clerks. He believed that those employees knew the customers' needs best of all and could make accurate and quick decisions about what would sell best. To support this process, each store was sent sales reports highlighting what had sold the day before, the day before that, and the top-selling items. Japan's 7-Elevens sell fresh food, so deliveries were made three times a day. Suzuki connected the clerks with the suppliers so that deliveries could be based on real-time data about immediate needs.[28] As a result, 7-Eleven in Japan has been its most profitable business for over thirty years—and its story is not about big data or complex systems or computer-generated numbers. It is about *empowering employees* to make their own decisions based on the range of data combined with their direct experience of serving customers on a daily basis.

Leaders of uplifting organizations and systems know the importance of using the right data and thorough evidence-informed decision making. They use *meaningful metrics* that connect indicators to core purposes, and that value personal experience and relationships alongside objective evidence as a basis for judgment. They measure what they value rather than valuing only what they can easily measure. The metrics are also meaningful because they include a broad range of relevant indicators, are made available for real-time tracking and response, and include long-range trend measures that guard against bullwhip effects. Tracking processes recognize the constant need to take the temperature of the organization and be informed about current progress by having access to just-in-time data.

Leaders of uplifting organizations and systems also set ambitious, stretch targets for improvement, based on the data they value. In many cases, they set these targets collaboratively so that everyone feels ownership for them. But in every event, they identify goals in the context of trusting and supportive relationships; targets are never imposed by a distant and uncaring bureaucracy.

Uplifting organizations and systems may think of themselves as being data-driven. But within these organizations, *people*—not the data—are driving the action. They value personal knowledge, strong relationships, and collective responsibility. They use data to support and stimulate them in the essentially social process of improvement, not as a low-cost substitute for human endeavor. Data cannot replace these core relationships that are the bedrock of success. They can, however, gently push and pull people in these relationships to focus their attention on the right things and to ensure that their efforts are put to good and lasting effect. We explore how these kinds of lasting effects produce sustainable success in the next chapter.

Chapter Six

Sustainable Success

With Janet Goodall

> *It is a common defect in men, not to consider in good weather the possibility of a tempest.*
>
> —Niccolo Machiavelli, The Prince (1452)

Staying Up

The core of uplifting leadership is *sustainability*. Unfortunately, sustainability is often an afterthought of organizational change. It is the unread postscript, the parting shot that nobody hears, the ripened fruit that's already starting to rot before it reaches its market. On the highway of attempted improvement, last-ditch efforts to secure sustainability are often the final truck stop before disappointment and remorse. Sustainability is the thing we think about when all the action has ended, when the good times are over and the money is all but spent. "This has been great," we say. "But how do we keep it going?"

The moment we ask this question, it's already too late. Things and people will already be moving on. The focus will almost certainly be shifting. There's still a long way to go, and you're rapidly running out of gas.

Sustainability should be one of the *first* things we think about, not the last.[1] What will we do when our investment runs out? Shall we stick with our original purposes, or grow as fast as we can? Who will replace us when we leave? How can we prepare everyone for that time? How long will I need to stay here to see things through? When will I have passed my sell-by date? How can we hit our short-term targets without sacrificing our long-term goals? Shall we keep on improving in what we're already good at, or strike out in a new direction instead? These are the essential and eternal questions of leadership in organizations, and they should be uppermost in our earliest efforts to change. The answers to these questions define our ability to turn initial success into sustainable improvement.

Nonsustainability

The opposite of sustainability is nonsustainability: the failure to improve or even to *exist* in the long haul. It is the Grim Reaper that stalks and often strikes down all efforts made towards change. Nonsustainability is evident not only in the end of existence, but also in the loss of core values and purposes that define the nature of that existence. Every factor of uplifting leadership that has emerged from our research can be upended by the impact of non-sustainability. Through our work, we've discovered three recurring features of nonsustainability that we discuss in the following sections.

1. False Starts and Recoveries

Nonsustainability occurs when people forget who they are and lose sight of what's important. It can happen to the best of us, as it did to Ron Toigo, president of and driving force behind the Vancouver Giants hockey organization. Toigo made his wealth developing real estate in Western Canada. As we sat in the director's box before the team's last game of the season, Toigo told us about his first failed hockey ownership venture back in the 1990s. As a fan of the sport with the funds to make a big investment, he decided he would like to own a team: "It's a business that has a scoreboard, so it's a lot more fun than most businesses," he recalled.

Toigo's first opportunity came along with a drive of several hours south to the Tri-City Americans hockey club. Looking back, he felt, it had been a disaster. The long drive to every game meant he had no connection to or passion for the community. It was just a team he had bought because he could. Whenever results dipped, they looked for quick and easy answers like trading for older players and giving up high-draft picks. "We didn't know who we were," he said. "We never got our head around deciding what we wanted to be. We just wanted to win." The team wasn't successful and the relationship didn't feel right, so he pulled out.

Toigo learned fast. His second investment effort was close to home, in Vancouver, where he felt he could find a purpose and a connection. But his city already had a hockey team—the high-flying Vancouver Canucks, 2011 finalists in the sport's Stanley Cup. Dale Saip, vice president in charge of business development, pointed out that the Giants are the only junior hockey team that is located in the same city as a pro NHL team and not owned by them. But this isn't a bad thing, he said. Instead of seeing the high-flying pro-Canucks as competitors, the Giants regard them as an opportunity and an ally. "You don't see a lot of children at Canuck games. We have season-ticket-holding families. The entire family is there every game and they're having a great time with it."

The Giants' on-ice identity is bold and brash, but off the ice it's a family organization through and through. So the Giants are the team that attracts families rather than corporate types. There are moments when this "higher love" for family, community, and hockey in general are obvious on the ice as well as off. As we sat behind the goals at the end of the thrilling final game of the regular season, the Giants' players lined up on center ice to give young fans the shirts off their backs in a ceremony that bonded players and fans together throughout the stadium. Toigo had found his team and his purpose, right in his own community. But he had to fight for its existence against the accepted wisdom that two hockey clubs in one town would be one too many. In the business of sports, false starts are common when you have an open checkbook and are in a rush for success. Sustainable development requires a different kind of investment—in the people and communities who matter to you.

Sometimes, a loss of purpose comes not at the moment of starting something up but during a downturn. In *How the Mighty Fall*, business guru Jim Collins describes how companies that fall from greatness sometimes experience, in the midst of their decline, a brief but false recovery.[2] Leading global retailer Marks & Spencer was one of them.

Marks & Spencer is a rags-to-riches story of how a Polish immigrant named Michael Marks teamed up with Thomas Spencer in 1894 to open the first of their company's market stalls in the North of England.[3] They grew steadily during the first hundred years, establishing stores throughout the United Kingdom. Marks & Spencer developed a reputation for selling high-quality products at reasonable prices with a no-quibble policy of exchanging goods when customers returned them. In 1998, they became the first British retailer to return a profit of over £1 billion. The company seemed to be firmly ensconced as the nation's favorite store.

By 2009, Marks & Spencer—eventually known as M&S—was the forty-third largest retailer in the world with 600 stores in Britain and 285 more spread across forty countries around the globe. It was rated the most reputable company out of 140 of the largest UK businesses.[4] M&S has also been a Global Sustainability Leader in retail on the Dow Jones Sustainability Index.[5]

Yet after more than a century of sustained success through and beyond the late 1990s, M&S experienced several years of volatile performance and managerial turmoil. The company's strong performance numbers were impressive—but also deceptive, because they masked an accumulating set of problems. On the one hand, many of the stores' idiosyncratic practices—such as not accepting credit cards or not providing changing rooms for customers—had become ridiculously outdated. In addition, confidence was turning into overconfidence in market and acquisition terms. Sir Richard Greenbury, who was CEO and Chairman of M&S in the late 1990s, rapidly expanded store space at home and overseas—which more than doubled the annual investment rate. Profit margins were pushed to untenable levels—something that was reflected in M&S's growing prices and diminishing quality of customer care. The company seemed to lose its customer focus and ended up producing "vast acres of gray" in its women's fashions that were not stylistically or commercially successful.[6]

The approach wasn't working, but the company only responded by driving the numbers harder and harder, seeking more and more profit. It was locked into a kind of summit fever that was coming at the cost of losing touch with its customers. In her account of the rise and fall of Marks & Spencer, Judi Bevan concludes that, "Greenbury and his colleagues pushed the business too far. . . . A little at a time they sacrificed the founding family principles of value, quality and service in the dash for profits."[7]

Emerging and expanding competition from UK retailers such as Primark, Next, and Tesco produced modern and competitively priced lines of clothing shown in attractive store displays. They also offered more flexible delivery as well as the use of store loyalty cards that were now standard in retail—something M&S did not do.[8]

The new millennium heralded a false recovery for M&S. They introduced online shopping, began accepting credit cards, and launched a new range of clothing. This temporarily improved profits and recovered some of M&S's market share. However, the new designers had no long-standing allegiance to M&S and they used their highly publicized success to move on. Results began to fall again and yet more takeover wrangles destabilized the organization. Marks & Spencer would need a better solution than temporary investments in new fashion lines and designers if it was going to secure more sustainable success. Later in the chapter, we'll take a look at the approach they took instead.

In a case study for Harvard Business School, Professors Robert Eccles, George Serafeim, and Kyle Armbrester describe the subsequent collapse. "The company's profits peaked in 1998 with revenues of £8.2 billion and an operating profit of £1.1 billion, but profits soon declined once again due to the continuing difficulty of using primarily British suppliers, and the eroding loyalty of customers who were torn between fidelity to the British-based company and the appeal of lower prices. The company's financial downfall was severe; its share price fell by more than two-thirds, and its operating profit plummeted to £145 million, with revenues of £8 billion in the financial year 2000/2001."[9]

2. Hubris and Complacency

Organizations can also start to become unsustainable when they take their achievements for granted and bathe too readily in the afterglow of their perceived success. Nonsustainability happens when confidence turns into overconfidence and earned pride descends into arrogance and hubris. Sustainable improvement is imperiled the moment leaders believe they have no more to learn and insulate themselves from critical feedback.

Cricket Australia faltered when its players developed a smug and superior attitude to their performance and invested their energy in personal distractions and contractual quibbling instead. Scott Bader faced financial difficulties when its employees prioritized the good causes to which they were contributing over the necessity to make a profit. Fiat Auto had to pull out of the

US market when its unreliable vehicles and unattractive designs no longer represented the stylish brand and reputation that had made the company popular in the 1960s.

When you forget to fight for what you believe in and stay connected to it, every day, in good times and bad, you can become cocooned and complacent and end up forfeiting everything that is important to you.

3. Killing the Competition

Organizations can also become unsustainable when they take dismissive and destructive approaches to their competitors. They either ignore or try to annihilate the competition. Like the Beatles' jealous song character, Rocky Raccoon, they may try to shoot off the legs of their rivals. Unsustainable organizations and their leaders do not respect their opponents. They underestimate them, try to eliminate them, or feel they have nothing to learn from them. They do not know how to combine competition with collaboration, which causes them to miss opportunities to advance.

The protection afforded by Fiat's dominance of its domestic market in the 1990s sheltered it from its declining performance in the increasingly important global market. Cricket Australia knew that it could only be financially viable off the field and consistently competitive on it if it helped to create a global financial infrastructure for its sport that would paradoxically make it less able to dominate the international competition with predictability. They knew that sports fans and media do not take well to teams whose disproportionately vast wealth can almost guarantee the annihilation of all opposition, game after game. And, as we saw in the case of software and cable providers in chapter 3, customers resist business monopolies that reduce customer choice and service in the sector to the one-size-fits-all levels of a Stalinist-type bureaucracy.

One obvious way to secure sustainable success is to avoid these pitfalls of nonsustainability. Ensure that you don't replace bold and inspiring dreams with the pursuit of performance numbers for their own sake. Never give up the fight for a better future. Play every game to the last minute. Do not blindly follow the herd. Discard invalid and inaccurate performance metrics. Resist the temptation to turn to individual heroes who you are tempted to believe will turn things around instantaneously and single-handedly. And instead of trying to destroy all opposition, join forces with your competitors when there is good to be done or something greater to be gained. These are surefire ways towards sustaining success and staying aloft.

However, we don't achieve success simply by avoiding bad practice. We get there by making deliberate decisions and taking positive actions designed to bring about sustainability. Finland is one place that brings these positive factors of sustainability together. Not only was Finland the highest performing country in the world (certainly outside Asia) on the PISA test indicators of student achievement for many years, but it also compares favorably to other countries in economic competitiveness, innovation, corporate transparency, and children's health and well-being.

Finnish Lessons

At 8 a.m. on a dark January morning in 2007, one of us boarded a train in Helsinki to travel to the municipal district of Jarvenpaa. Andy was part of a three-person work team assembled by the Organization for Economic Cooperation and Development (OECD)—an international policy body that influences government directions in global and national educational strategies—to determine some of the reasons why Finland was then the world leader on OECD's international PISA tests in student achievement.[10]

In 2010, three Asian jurisdictions—Hong Kong, Shanghai, and Singapore—were added, and Finland still remained the highest performing country outside them. Therefore, it was still the leader on the original list of countries. In equity terms, compared to other PISA participants, Finland also has the lowest variation between schools—just one-tenth of the OECD average. This means that unlike countries such as the United States and England, it is nearly impossible to predict a Finnish child's educational performance based on how much wealth that child's parents possess, or on what they do for a living.[11]

One of the schools we visited in Jarvenpaa was just two miles from the home of famous classical Finnish composer Jean Sibelius.[12] One indicator of its characteristic creativity is the fact that Finland has more orchestral composers per capita than any other developed country. Jarvenpaa's Upper Secondary School typifies the modern design features of most of the country's schools. A group of Finnish students showed us how they combined traditional artistic creativity with technology through computer-based graphic design, and were equally proud of their work with more traditional media in paint and textiles.

Creativity is a national priority in these schools; it reaffirms what it means to be Finnish. All of the country's students study creative and performing arts until the end of high school with musical instruments paid for by the state. Technological creativity and competitiveness do not break Finns from their past; instead, they connect the people to their history in a coherent narrative of lifelong learning and development of the whole society.

The reasons for this emphasis on creativity also came from a crisis. In the early 1990s, the country was hit by an economic catastrophe. There had been excessive property speculation at the time, and in 1992, the bubble had finally burst. Worse still, the collapse of the Soviet Union in 1991 had meant the end of a captive market for Finnish products such as paper and rubber. The impact on Finland's economy was cataclysmic. Unemployment rates rose to almost 20 percent and public debt stood at over 60 percent of gross domestic product (GDP).

Prime Minister Aho and his government took the emergency step of devaluing the Finnish currency to boost exports, but this was just a stop-gap measure. They would need to instigate a bolder, longer-term approach as well. In his book *Finnish Lessons*, Harvard Professor Pasi Sahlberg—formerly director of Finland's Center for International Mobility—describes how the economic crisis brought together the nation's political leaders to join those from the universities and from the corporate world to define an inspiring dream that would galvanize the whole nation.[13]

These leaders turned to the best resource they had: the country's people. Finland believed it could have a creative and prosperous future if it became an advanced knowledge economy that could respond quickly to and invent its way out of any future crisis. To do this, they would need to equip future generations with the relevant knowledge and skills that would surpass any they might purchase elsewhere in the world. So the Finns set about designing a creative, high-skill, high-wage knowledge economy in which people invent, apply, share, and circulate knowledge at a higher level and faster pace than all competitors.

This made it necessary for them to continue expanding and investing in high-quality education, with high-quality teaching for everyone. It involved no quick fixes. In Finland, a strong public education system provides education free of charge as a universal right all the way through school and higher education. Private education is almost nonexistent. All teachers possess master's degrees; the acceptance rate into teacher education programs stands at less than 10 percent; and the inspiring dream that assigns national importance to education and educators draws the brightest and most committed graduates into teaching. Indeed, teaching is one of the top two professions that people look for in future marriage partners. (The top choice for future husbands, on which we pass no comment, is medical doctors!)

Finland's high-quality education promotes innovation. Almost 3 percent of GDP is allocated to scientific and technological development—higher than any other developed country. About half of Finland's primary teachers have taken mathematics or science as their major or minor subject in university. But innovation and creativity aren't restricted to science and technology. Just as we saw in Jarvenpaa, they are infused throughout the school curriculum and connected to Finns' traditional identity as a creative nation of artisans.

The Finnish dream has been an inclusive and inspiring one. It has been steered from the center, but driven by people's sense of collective responsibility in their own local communities. It reinvents and reaffirms people's common identity from the past to yield spectacular economic and educational results in the present and the future—assigning high status to education and bringing outstanding and well-trained graduates into it. According to Professor Sahlberg, this dream has managed to "survive opposing political governments and ministries unharmed and intact."[14]

As we first mentioned in chapter 2, the Finns have pursued their great national dream in their characteristic spirit of *sisu*: to persist despite all obstacles. When the Finns set out to improve their educational system, their priority was not pushing and stretching gifted students at the top. Rather, it was to lift up *each* child, one by one, from the bottom. This is why Finland's special educational strategy applies to almost any child who struggles with part of their learning.[15] By the time they have finished upper secondary school, about half of all Finnish students will have been designated as having a special educational need at one point or another. Support is available within the class, then from in-class assistants, and then by other provision if necessary. Each school has a welfare team that meets weekly to discuss any potentially struggling students. This attention to equity did not get instant results across the country. However, by raising the prospects of every child and then improving the climate of all classrooms as fewer and fewer students were falling behind, the bar at the top began to lift, year after year.

It became evident in the 2013 announcements of the PISA results that Finland's performance had fallen back a little.[16] This has raised questions about whether Finns—like the iconic Finnish telecommunications company Nokia, which makes up a large part of the national economy—have become a little too complacent about the Finnish Way of change that has served the nation so well for twenty years.[17] Indeed, when we have returned to Finland ourselves to report on our work and asked Finns what their dream is for the next twenty years, the most common response has been "to keep it just as it is."

However, since the early 1990s, Finland's economic and educational reforms have demonstrated the importance of three aspects of sustainability:

- They **laid firm foundations for change** in a strong public system that connected future goals to traditionally valued identities.
- They pursued **improvement** at a **feasible growth rate**.
- They **connected short-term gains to long-term goals**, instead of seeking large and early spikes in economic performance and student achievement.

The Finns understood these important elements of sustainable success: that it must stand on something solid; grow at a rate that is neither too slow to maintain momentum nor too fast to burn everyone out; and avoid the temptations of false recoveries by linking short-term gains to long-term goals.

Let's look at each of these elements in more detail.

1. Firm Foundations

The seemingly sudden and spectacular impact of heroic leadership and meteoric success is often underpinned by years of foundation building by others. Their efforts have halted previous decline, developed better business models, built new relationships, or created new infrastructures of financial, physical, and human resources.

Charismatic leaders are often only able to exert an impact by standing on the shoulders of unsung yet quietly effective heroes who went before them. In the London borough of Tower Hamlets, former director Christine Gilbert built on the firm foundations laid down by her otherwise unheard-of predecessor, Anne Sofer. Indeed, the improvement in test results from 1997 to 2000 under Gilbert's publicly acclaimed leadership was identical to the rate of improvement from 1994 to 1997 during Sofer's initial leadership. Sofer had established clear structures and financial efficiency out of chaos, which served as a secure platform for Gilbert to undertake her own initiatives. Gilbert successfully followed on from Sofer, and passed on to Kevan Collins who followed Gilbert in turn, each one building on and adding to the achievements of their predecessor to gain further uplift. The sustained success by students in their schools is confirmed by the Tower Hamlets story published in 2013.[18]

Many high performers on the international PISA tests of student achievement are blessed with political stability, so that education policy is not driven from one election to the next by short-term political priorities that are often the opposite of the ones that were implemented by the government before. Finland, for example, mainly places educational policy above party political differences. The high-performing Canadian province of Alberta has had the same party (Conservatives) in control for forty years, and thus it can plan with some certainty and continuity from one election to the next. And although Singapore is a democracy in principle, in practice it has been a one-party state.

If there is no continuity or progression in the system, it must be established by individual leaders themselves. Gianni Agnelli laid the foundations for Sergio Marchionne at Fiat by returning the focus back to the auto sector as its core operation at a time when Fiat had been involved in a wide range of acquisitions outside its own sector. Adrian Lim was able to pursue technologically driven innovation at Ngee Ann Secondary School, because, as he fully appreciated, his predecessors had established a solid platform of achievement and results before him. Ontario's Liberal government could undertake its highly acclaimed literacy reforms, not because it started with nothing, but because it already had a strong and capable teaching force that had simply become disillusioned under the previous top-down government.

Few successful leaders start with a blank slate. There is often more to their predecessors and what they have achieved than immediately meets the eye. Sustainable success often comes about not by eradicating preceding leaders from history or memory, but by connecting the dots between achievements that they've accomplished.

One way to make these connections, and to perpetuate a legacy of uplifting leadership is through a process we call "prodigal leadership." The prodigal leader is like the prodigal son in the Bible who is welcomed home to the family after many years away. A number of prodigal leaders in our study had spent formative years of their career in the organization where they developed lasting loyalties to it. They then went away to gather outside experience that added other important insights and dimensions to their leadership, and eventually returned with a powerful blend of insider-outsider perspectives. Burnley Football Club's Chairman Barry Kilby had once played for the club's youth team. A number of Cricket Australia's executives used to be high-level players for their states. Tricia Okoruwa started work as a teacher in Tower Hamlets, left for a while to teach abroad, and returned to Hackney as a teacher leader, then progressed to principal, eventually stepping up to become director of education.

An especially interesting case of prodigal leadership concerned Marks & Spencer's Sir Stuart Rose. When Rose became chairman of M&S in 2004, he made many urgent closures and selloffs—such as financial services to HSBC bank—that were the company's quick wins. But Rose's childhood experiences of living in a trailer on the brink of poverty had convinced him of the importance of maintaining a solid foundation.[19] His more basic impetus was to rebuild—persistently and relentlessly.

Rose reconnected M&S to his earlier experiences. He had joined the company as an executive trainee and stayed for seventeen years, ingesting the organization's culture. He then moved away to take a promotion with another retail competitor. He was the insider-outsider leader who came from afar and also from below. According to a store manager, "People were at low ebb and they looked towards Stuart Rose to take us out of the valley of death." A middle-level manager added that "Stuart understood the importance of a clear vision and a business plan that focused on product first and profit second."

Rose had a resounding view of innovation, "Leading customers is also important. If you wait for customers to tell you that you need to do something, you're too late. Good business leaders should be half a step ahead of what customers want, i.e., they don't actually quite know they want it. That's what innovation is about."[20] He continued, "There are always chief executives who are ahead of the game, who recognize that the world is not the place it was ten years ago and that they have to find different routes and listen to different inputs. They are in the minority."

Rose was clear about what M&S stood for: traditional, century-old values of price and quality. But while he retained the company's traditional values and qualities, Rose stressed the importance of changing practices. "Listen to your customers and respond quickly. Be true to your brand values but don't be proud and don't hang on to yesterday's way of doing things. If you do, you may not be around tomorrow."[21] For instance, Rose bravely emphasized environmental sustainability and ethical checks on the sourcing of products. His *Look Behind the Label* marketing campaign highlighted the ethical and environmental aspects of the production and sourcing methods that M&S engaged in. He championed new practices such as recycling of plastic bottles and reduction of plastic bags that persisted after his departure. He felt it was the company's duty to take these on for "compelling commercial as well as moral reasons," despite an 18 percent fall in share price during the onset of the global economic collapse.[22] These indicators of reputation and sustainability are now more important to M&S than achieving the highest quarterly returns imaginable or becoming the biggest retailer in the world.

Rose and his fellow leaders were not distracted by summit fever or by the lure of false recoveries. Instead, they concentrated on establishing the firm foundations of a compelling and morally grounded vision, and on making an inspiring connection of a sustainable future to the best of M&S's classic and long beloved past. In many ways, these emphases were embodied in Rose's own identity as a prodigal leader who came back to M&S to take it onwards and upwards.

In the years following the global economic collapse, many British consumers moved downstream in search of cheaper purchasing options. In addition, M&S has found itself in a constant struggle to retain and regain its standing and branding in the retail sector. The company's chances of success and sustainability will be determined by how well it fights for its core vision—and how, like Burberry's trench coats, it can stay connected to its classic heritage in ways that address the tastes and preferences of new generations of customers.

Even in seriously underperforming organizations, eliminating what all existing leadership has stood for is not always desirable—or even necessary. In *Change Without Pain*, author Eric Abrahamson advises against the turnaround tendency "to obliterate the past to create the future."[23] This, he says, leads to wild swings of the pendulum, increased employee burnout, and loss of collective expertise and memory. Instead, Abrahamson proposes, it is often better to creatively reunite existing capacity—"reusing, redeploying and recombining" people and teams in novel and more productive ways that.[24] Many of the high-performing organizations we analyzed had previous leaders that carefully laid the groundwork for uplifting leadership. These individuals had been around for some time, knew the organization and its culture well, and provided opportunities for growth.

Many of Hackney's head teachers were carefully groomed internally after unsuccessful efforts to import school leaders from outside. Scott Bader changed some of its executives but also deliberately hung on to many of the staff who defined its culture and its customer relations. And in Singapore and Canada, leaders like Adrian Lim are constantly moved from the schools to the Ministry and back again so that they know the organizations they have to lead from within.

A house that is built on sand will not stay standing for long. And an organization without firm foundations has little chance of being sustainable either. No one creates something from absolutely nothing. All of us stand on the shoulders of someone whose efforts preceded ours. Acknowledging our predecessors' work and creating platforms for further achievement by our successors are the only ways we can all eventually put the roof on our collective achievements, long after many of us have departed.

2. Feasible Growth

Another element of sustainable success involves the rates at which organizations grow. Beyond the swift actions necessary to counter any initial crisis, uplifting organizations and their leaders don't try to expand as quickly as possible or take off too fast. They are built on gradual and deliberate growth. They show practical and prudent attention to growth rates that do not compromise the future by improving or expanding too quickly in the present—or by making excessive investments, overrelying on imported stars, or pushing staff to the point of burnout.

Two companies in our study that grasped the essential rule of feasible growth are the relatively newly established businesses of Dogfish Head Craft Brewery and Shoebuy.com. The standard practice of microbreweries in the 1990s was, in the words of Vice President Mariah Calagione, to "secure investment of around $5 million and [get] this really shiny, copper, beautiful system and put it in like a façade window at their brewery." But as a result, she said, "most of those breweries did not survive." Had Dogfish Head done that at the time, she concluded, "there's no way we could have afforded to pay for it. So we scrapped it together." Dogfish Head owner Sam Calagione doesn't want "to be ashamed of the fact that we had to start on shitty dairy and canning equipment because our ethos was all about innovation. And innovation meant doing everything you could with limited resources to actually make something." Dogfish started slowly, and has grown at a rate that it can control. This is why, up until now, it has resisted exporting to Canada and overseas—so that it doesn't have to sacrifice quality for growth.

Shoebuy.com has had similar preoccupations. One of the reasons the company was able to survive the dot-com bust just after its establishment was because it didn't leverage venture capital investment at the outset. Many companies were able to raise large amounts of money with relative ease during the build-up to the dot-com bubble via venture capitalists who were hoping to reap huge profits from the advent of the Internet. But the majority of these investors emphasized short-term gains and rapid growth, directed towards the financial attraction of going public on the stock market; thus, their investments came with all kinds of strings attached. Shoebuy consciously chose a more prudent path, because it wanted to hang on to its own purposes and control its own growth rate. Shoebuy leaders knew they wanted to grow their business aggressively but in ways that ensured long-term success. Not acquiring initial venture capital meant less money to play with at the beginning; however, it also ensured that they kept control of the company's focus and direction.

All the schools and school systems we have encountered raised achievement scores not by "teaching to the test" or working only with students close to the passing mark, but by authentically changing teaching and learning for the better with relentlessness and persistence. The resulting scores showed steady gains almost every year, rather than miraculous turnarounds in immediate results.

3. The Long and Short of Improvement

A third factor explaining sustainable success has been these organizations' ability to connect short-term gains to long-term success. In their investigation of four decades of financial data from over a thousand companies, business consultants Dominic Dodd and Ken Favaro found that "the stock market doesn't seem to value the ability to produce consecutive uninterrupted runs of positive earnings results."[25] Indeed, they found, slightly more sporadic performers do better in the long term. Sustainable success does not privilege short-term heroic targets, quarterly returns, and instant turnarounds above all else. The authors' results show that "the market rewarded companies that were better than average at achieving both short-term earnings and long-term economic profits" and were more able to reconcile "today and tomorrow."[26]

John Kotter, former professor at Harvard Business School and best-selling author of business books on leadership and change, took up social psychologist Karl Weick's original idea on the value of "small wins" or "quick wins." Kotter stressed that short-term, measurable improvements that build confidence and credibility must "make sure that visible results lend sufficient credibility to the (long-term) transformation effort."[27] Short-term turnaround efforts often fail to grasp this fundamental fact because they disconnect quick wins from the long-term goals they are supposed to serve. In order to secure sustainability, it is essential that team members not only understand the links between the long and short term—but can also strategically connect them. The London borough of Hackney captured this with two phrases: "find and fix" and "predict and prevent."

Hackney's Deputy Director Tricia Okoruwa and her team of consultants were in danger of being overwhelmed by their schools' needs. As school after school failed its inspection, the team was rushing around patching up schools just enough to scrape through next time. Okoruwa soon realized this strategy was unsustainable;

as they still had to go back later to support these schools properly. So Okoruwa separated them into two approaches she labeled "find and fix" and "predict and prevent." "Find and fix" strategies dealt with the short-term issues like a weakness in grade 3 in one school or in writing at grade 6 in another. Coaches were sent in to work with schools on specific shortcomings like this, allowing them to gain quick wins. "Predict and prevent" were the long-term strategies that included investing heavily in the early years before the children had fallen behind. These measures yielded strong results down the line on the national tests at age eleven. This allowed Hackney to address the long- and short-term together.

Short-term "quick wins" are important, but not if they distract from enduring goals and core purposes. Through investing in its National Center for Excellence and diverting some resources from the immediate interests of the current elite team to do this, Cricket Australia develops a sense of who will be its future national team captains or leaders, almost from childhood. Fiat more than halved its automobile production schedule; however, it also concentrated immense collective energy on ensuring that this would not put product quality or customer safety at risk. Dogfish Head beer doesn't want to shoot off the legs of its big beer rivals, but wants to grow enough to begin to affect drinkers' ideas about the nature of good beer. Shoebuy.com is "metric obsessed"; yet the Internet models that the company develops are "scalable" and sustainable.

Short-term wins *are* crucial. Scott Bader nearly went out of existence because it ignored this bottom line of business. And as economist John Maynard Keynes accurately pointed out, "In the long run, we're all dead."[28] But the indicators and achievements that matter right now cannot be all that matters. They have to be consistent with the dreams and visions that businesses, sports teams, and educational organizations pursue for their customers, families, and future fans. That is the long and short of sustainable change.

Conclusion

Uplifting people needn't mean uprooting them. The paradox of uplifting leadership is that it also has to stand on firm ground. You cannot lift each other up if you are on a shaky foundation. Sustainable success requires a solid footing, as well as a manageable rate of progress and an ability and willingness to ensure that immediate actions are connected to long-term results. In 1987, the Brundtland Report of the World Commission on Environment and Development defined the essence of sustainable development as the ability "to meet the needs of the present without compromising the ability of future generations to meet their own needs."[29]

This is the ultimate ambition of uplift—to improve the prospects of the generations who will succeed you long after you are gone, while making sure that you can make things better for the people you lead and serve in the present. And that requires action—which we now turn to in the final chapter.

Chapter Seven

Uplifting Action

If the highest aim of a captain were to preserve his ship, he would keep it in port forever.

—*Saint Thomas Aquinas*

The Quest for Uplift

How do start-ups succeed and then sustain their success? How do organizations turn themselves around from the depths of failure or bring themselves back from the edge of extinction and then stay turned around after that? How is it possible to transform the educational results of large systems and whole societies, rather than in one or two schools at the expense of their neighbors? And how do leaders succeed when they face exceptionally challenging circumstances or have to operate with meager support compared to their peers?

Our detailed examination of fifteen organizations across three sectors in eight countries highlighted the way that leaders responded to various challenges by taking their organizations and communities on an uplifting quest that raised their performance, their people, and themselves to significantly higher levels.

We found that uplifting leadership identifies and articulates a real but improbable destination or dream to aim for at the outset. It creates a bracing sense of trepidation that prompts the desire to move to a better place. It connects future aspirations to classic origins in a way that affirms people's sense of who they are and what they feel called to do. Pursuing this dream also involves a determined and relentless struggle to succeed in the face of formidable obstacles and challenges.

Uplifting leadership then takes uncommon routes that go under the radar or into the storm, embracing paths that others may have overlooked or even avoided. It takes off into the wind using opposing forces and resistance as resources to create elevation, and it uses competition to stimulate and strengthen the collective force of collaboration.

Throughout the journey, uplifting leadership pushes and pulls people forward. Trust and teamwork draw people along toward inspiring goals and through engaging work and relationships. Vibrant teams also push each other upward as peers engage in spirits of friendly rivalry and act with collective responsibility to keep on outdoing each other in pursuit of better performance and the achievement of a higher purpose.

Uplifting leadership is able to connect the present's urgent demands to the importance of reaching a desirable long-term future by using navigational tools that keep people on course. It motivates them in their quest by marking how far they have progressed and noting the distance they still have to go.

Finally, uplifting leadership is launched from a firm foundation and solid platform for departure. It adopts and utilizes viable business models, efficient organizational structures, high-trust relationships, and effective leadership succession. It proceeds at a sustainable pace that does not exceed capacity, waste resources, lose connection with core purposes, or wear people out.

Each of these six factors encompasses inner tensions that leaders are adept at holding together. Uplifting leadership is hard and soft, in that it requires inspiration and dogged determination. It involves playful creativity that is also prepared to face up to opposing currents of opinion. It embraces both collaboration and competition, pushes and also pulls people forward. And it is able to reconcile long-term sustainability with short-term success.

This is the quest of uplifting leadership—one that elevates everyone and their performance to a higher level. But the uplifting quest also requires a particular kind of character that is able to achieve collective elevation without gratuitous or self-indulgent senses of elation.

Elevation, Not Elation

Uplifting leadership, like all leadership, begins with the self. In his groundbreaking work on the psychiatry of leadership, *The Leader on the Couch*, Manuel Kets de Vries argues that "if we want things to be different, we must start by being different ourselves."[1] If you cannot lead yourself, it's likely you will be unable to lead anyone else for long. De Vries brilliantly portrays many of the clinical pathologies of leaders who read like a parade of characters from Bob Dylan's "Desolation Row"—narcissistic, controlling, depressive, dramatic, and paranoid leaders.[2] And among them is one leadership type that might easily be confused with uplifting leadership—the hypomanic charismatic leader who thrives on emotional elation.

German sociologist Max Weber was the first to put forward the idea of charismatic authority almost a century ago. Weber explained it as a form of authority that rests not on bureaucratic rules, like a government department, nor on traditions and rituals, like a tribe or a church, but on special gifts that certain individuals possess that make people want to follow them.[3] The Greeks called this *kharisma*. Vision, energy, charm, magnetism, optimism, self-belief, daring, flamboyance, and enthusiasm—these are the qualities that often draw people to charismatic leaders.

Of course, this particular kind of leader can be a good influence or a bad one, depending on the ends that are pursued. Bill Clinton and Tony Blair are classic examples of charismatic leaders; so too are Adolf Hitler and Eva Perón. But even when the intentions are honorable and the ends are worthy, the upbeat attributes of charismatic leadership can still be excessive. Elation can be easily confused with elevation, turning a motivating culture into a mindless cult—with delusional and disastrous results. Heroic CEOs have sometimes led their companies into grandiose mergers and acquisitions that end up in insolvency. Gung-ho educational reformers can tear their systems and people apart with one unfinished initiative after another. And defiant sports coaches can stubbornly insist that the team's mood is good and that every game has its "positives" even after a string of abject performances and results.

People who lead like this may well be psychopaths, says leadership development expert Manuel Kets De Vries. He writes of how psychopathic leaders are like the real-life character Jordan Belfort depicted in the 2013 movie *The Wolf of Wall Street*. Belfort reached "astonishing heights" but "conned his way through life," showing "complete disregard for others" and "ending up in jail for fraud."[4] The only thing that matters to psychopathic leaders, says De Vries, is winning—and as their "impression management" skills get them to the top, they wreak havoc on the organization and other people's lives along the way.

Uplifting leadership isn't just about being positive or self-confident. Uplifting leaders aren't "up" for their own sake to get or give a constant emotional fix, or to bolster self-importance. And they are not so insistent on always having a positive spin, that, in De Vries' words, they are "willing to sacrifice the truth on the altar of intimacy."[5]

In his cleverly titled book, *The Antidote: Happiness for People Who Can't Stand Positive Thinking*, Oliver Burkeman warns against taking a superficial, cheerleading approach to making ourselves or others deliberately happier by articulating positive thoughts, boosting self-esteem, or articulating best-case scenarios.[6] *Trying* to be happy doesn't usually make us happy, says Burkeman—just like wanting to be Number 1 rarely gets us to Number 1. Paradoxically, Burkeman explains, we can become happier if we actually contemplate and decide that we can live with the worst-case scenario. Indeed, we will be pleasantly surprised when things eventually turn out better than we expected. According to Burkeman, happiness and success depend just as much on stoic qualities of perseverance, self-sacrifice, and bearing up under pressure—or on quiet states of meditation and reflection—as they do on upbeat expressions of positive thoughts.

Therefore, uplifting leadership isn't the same as *inspirational* leadership—with its rousing speeches and calls to arms to achieve a noble purpose that everyone can embrace. Nor is it equivalent to *transformational* leadership, with its inspiring visions and directions and its capacity to bind people together in the joy and challenge of an energizing and engaging quest. If leadership is invested only in the emotional highs that come from positive, self-determined, inspiring, and mutually absorbing work, then it can just as easily lead people like lemmings to their doom as it can lift them up to greatness.

Uplifting leadership embraces many of the positive and optimistic attributes of inspirational and transformational leadership, but it also includes additional and even opposing qualities that it's somehow able to hold together simultaneously. Uplifting leaders know how to convert dreams into action. They thrive on good feelings, but also feed off the accomplishment of a good result. They know that charismatic inspiration comes to nothing unless accompanied by toil, tenacity, and perspiration. Innovation must be disciplined if it is to be effective. But discipline alone can suck the soul out of an organization. So creative engagement and enjoyment have to be part of the mix too. A twenty-first-century set of "soft skills" such as risk taking and creativity needs to be counterbalanced by 1950s virtues of honesty, integrity, and plain, hard work. An uplifting mindset and skill set keeps your head up high while your feet stay firmly planted on the ground.

Whether they are ordinary or extraordinary individuals, uplifting leaders acknowledge the unsung predecessors who have laid the groundwork before them. They construct platforms to help elevate others in bringing forth and sharing their leadership as well. Indeed, like Sam and Mariah Calagione at Dogfish Head Craft Brewery, the strongest leaders are those who are most able to let go of some of their own power and to create spaces where others' decisions can come to fruition.

Down to Earth

So how does your community or organization achieve uplift? Where does everyone begin? In the words of Mahatma Gandhi, "you have to be the change you want to see in others"—that is, you must start with yourself.[7] This final chapter will apply the six factors of uplifting leadership to help you identify practical, down-to-earth implications for improving your own performance and the performance of the people around you.

1. Dreaming with Determination

Dare to Dream. The first step is to develop and articulate an inspiring dream that *you all share.* This cannot be something that's reduced to a number or a ranking or a mission statement. Before you decide how high you want to get, you need to ask, "What do you want to *be?*" So rouse yourself to dream big in ways that fit your own context and world view. Perhaps you can change people's relationship with health and food, or give working class and ethnic minority children as good a chance in school as anyone else's child. Maybe you want to be able to raise the status of sports for women, or indigenous groups, or people with disabilities, in your own community.

Your success is not limited by your current ability. You will grow and develop along the way—but in order to do so, you need to raise your aspirations first. Even if you don't quite reach the improbable goals you set, you will exceed the modest ones you once thought were far too ambitious. But be sure to separate the downright impossible from the upright improbable. Chase an *inspiring dream*, not an indulgent fantasy or an idle wish. Encourage yourself with stories of people who have achieved what you want to emulate. But remember you are unique and that your way will be different from theirs. You can't rent or borrow goals from other people's models or strategies. They have to be owned by your own community.

Bring the Dream Alive. Uplifting leadership calls for great and inspiring storytelling by yourself and those around you. It includes myths of where you came from, epics about the obstacles you have surmounted, acknowledgments of the ancestors who inspired and paved the way for the quest you are pursuing, and exhortations to reach the future that lies ahead. Use these stories to reconnect people to the best of what they used to be. Remind them where you started together, how far you have come, and what work you must still do. Provide opportunities for people to share their personal testimonies of transformation. Show images that link your finest traditions with your boldest ambitions. Celebrate success but also keep striding ahead. Encourage your people ceaselessly. Communicate with them incessantly in daily conversations as well as grandstand presentations. Start every meeting by recognizing someone's recent accomplishment and remind everyone of how it contributes to the dream—but don't always commend the same few people. Ring a bell when you have all reached a valued sales or production target on the way to the dream. When you walk around your building, catch people doing things that support the dream and in just a sentence or a phrase say things like "see, all children can succeed," or "this puts us one vital step closer to achieving our goal."

Be Neither Fearful Nor Fearless. Uplifting leaders know that fear can either paralyze you with inaction or push you to excel.

Even when everything seems hopeless, it's better to try something than nothing. There's always the chance that your effort will miss the mark, of course—but in the words of legendary ice hockey player Wayne Gretzky, "You miss 100% of the shots you don't take."[8] Acknowledge your fears—but do not broadcast them. Explore them with mentors, coaches, partners, and friends, by all means, but do not wallow in self-pity and self-doubt in front of all your team. In the spirit of Rudyard Kipling, "If you can keep your head when all about you are losing theirs and blaming it on you," then you will lead yourself and others onward and upward.[9]

Fight for What's Right. Uplift rarely comes without struggle. Sometimes you will have to fight off competitors or opponents. But mainly, it is a higher cause that is most worth fighting for. Express righteous indignation when you witness injustice, but never be outrageous for its own sake. Learn from setbacks, and redouble your efforts in response. Richard Pirsig describes this brilliantly in his classic book *Zen and the Art of Motor Cycle Maintenance*.[10] When a bolt sheers off in the middle of trying to repair your motorcycle, try to view it not as an interruption to your repair work, but as just one more moment in the process. Struggle is part of leadership, not an interruption to it. So, overcome anxiety with deliberate, positive action. Realize that what you're dreading most can be the one thing that spurs you to move ahead. Understand that when higher purposes are at stake, most fights will be long. Do not promise or expect instant success. Whenever you feel tired, take a breather and cool down, then reignite yourself by remembering your purpose and your dream and the future of all the people who will prosper from it.

Acknowledge Others' Fears. Listen to and understand the fears of those around you: fear of failure, of change, of losing their jobs and their livelihoods. Never trivialize or minimize anxieties by comparing them with something even worse. It really doesn't help to be reminded in the midst of suffering that there's always someone worse off. Acknowledge the gravity of the situation, but be as positive as you can about finding a way forward. When there is a crisis—a hurricane, an explosion, or a financial collapse, perhaps—be the first to show up alongside your people and the first to speak up for them and to them. When tragedy strikes, statesmanlike presence that also demonstrates empathic engagement with people's confusion or suffering is the top priority of uplifting leadership.

2. Creativity and Counter-Flow

Use Surprise Tactics. Strategically, the power of surprise can set opponents off balance. Arreguin-Toft's book *How Weak Armies Win Wars* quotes Chairman Mao Tse-Tung regarding guerrilla warfare: "Select the tactic of seeming to come from the east and attacking from the west. Avoid the solid, attack the hollow. Withdraw when he advances; harass him when he stops; strike him when he is weary; pursue him when he withdraws."[11] In other words, do the *exact opposite* of what others expect if it will achieve the right results. Try to outthink and outflank a more powerful opponent. Praise those who oppose you; embrace the oncoming wind that gives you more swing.

Surprise Yourself. One of life's most underrated emotions is surprise. Shocks upset us, but surprises are sources of unexpected discovery and delight. They spark the curiosity and all-absorbing sense of uplift. So use your imagination. Try something different. This may be the paradoxical moment when it is time to change the game after enjoying years of success. You are likely to be more uplifted by an engaging innovation than by an incremental improvement.

Actively encourage disagreement and resistance. Invite your skeptics to join your team in the earliest stages of change. They won't hesitate to cite all the reasons why it might fail—so learning from them will help you avoid problems later on. There is also a chance that potential resisters will be motivated by their early participation, and that they might come to share your goals with you—spreading them out through their networks that you have little contact or credibility with yourself. Recognize that disagreement is also the lifeblood of creativity, but handle it in an agreeable way. Urge people to experiment. Share opportunities that stimulate innovation and promote creative autonomy in others. Tap into the diverse talents of your people. Do not surround yourself with clones. When you are faced with a seemingly insurmountable but unavoidable problem, use all the brainpower in your organization to identify and offset potential risks.

Trail Your Errors. Unlike the Apollo 13 mission, do make failure an option—but don't allow failures to turn into catastrophes. Although there is no innovation without some degree of failure, people cannot be held hostage to experimental excess. Eccentricity may conceive and give birth to an innovation; but it takes discipline to scale innovations up. Innovate on a small scale first with a few customers, or in just one or two classes in a school, or in a lower stakes game, before you go into the playoff finals, gear up to higher stakes, or spread out systemwide. Trial and error is the essence of creativity. But you must also track your errors through real-time data and metrics to prevent veering off too far in the wrong direction. Innovation must be squared with the evidence. Inquire into your innovations so that you can learn quickly from your mistakes and refine things relentlessly.

3. Collaboration with Competition

Give Away Your Best Ideas. Doing so will make it necessary to keep inventing new ones. Secure your intellectual property, but don't cling to it so possessively that it is no use to anyone else. When you gain an advantage that works, share it with your adversaries afterwards. Coach your opponents; have lunch with your rivals; help other people's children as well as your own. It will lift up the competition and force you to keep stretching yourself. Selflessness is the superego of self-interest, and it will make you all the stronger.

Lift Up a Competitor. Invest in your opponents, and hold out a hand when they have fallen. Encouraging other people helps to raise the standard of performance for everyone—including you—by expanding the market, increasing the quality of skills, or developing the entire community's level of learning.

Respect Your Rivals. Give your adversaries credit by acknowledging their success. Enjoy your victories but never try to annihilate your opponents. Destroying the competition completely will ultimately restrict your own growth. Friendly but fierce rivalry raises everyone's performance. Monopolies do not only breed resentment; they also feed complacency.

Benchmark Relentlessly. Build up a clear picture of how your competitors go about their work. The goal is to learn from them, not to leapfrog them. Use these comparisons to compete with your own previous best performance, not to diminish or destroy someone else's superior success. Try to adapt what you learn to suit your own situation rather than trying to imitate them. Learn from *many* rivals, not just one; this will challenge you to create your own superior solutions. Send people out to learn overseas and keep bringing visitors in from other systems. This will keep the learning constantly bubbling and circulating rather than have you always searching for internal solutions.

Seek Higher Common Ground. Find ways to collaborate with your competitors for mutual benefit and greater good. Work together off the field, even as you compete on it. Cooperate and federate when you become aware that your collective efforts can serve a greater good. Make the first move in approaching your rivals; don't wait for the initiative to come from them.

4. Pushing and Pulling

Know Your People. Be more concerned about your people's welfare than you are about your own. Be very visible on the surface of a lot of things, rather than in the depths of a few things. Get as close as possible to as many people as you can—but don't suffocate them with inescapable attention. Know people's names and learn things about their lives. Get out of your office and meet people. Spend time with the workers, the cleaners, and your customers. They will give you the clearest sense of how you are doing, and the strongest reminder that everyone is contributing to the effort. Get on to the assembly line, out into classrooms, and into the locker rooms. Walk the floors. This is where your people are. This is how you know what they do and what their working lives are like. You don't need an excuse to do someone else's job for a day, to walk in their shoes and appreciate their contribution.

Draw the Best out of Your Teams. Understand that some teams and their leaders will get off to a slow or rocky start. If you have known your people for a long time, you will know who can lead, even if they cannot do it right away. If reliable people have been performing poorly in one role, take responsibility for helping them to improve. Recombine and redeploy people before you think about replacing them. But don't be governed by sentiment. Know and acknowledge your own weaknesses. Team up with people who can compensate for them. Help people to learn more about each other. In sports, try changing positions in play; in business, try working in a different section; and in education, switch to another class, grade, or school. Encourage interplay and interchange of roles and positions. You will learn more together and lift each other up.

Build Trust. If you invest your time in building trust, it will pay dividends down the line. It is easier to challenge people who trust you than it is to trust people whom you have only ever been confrontational with previously. Have faith in someone to watch your back, and watch their back too. Understand that trust takes time to be verified through many interactions; but once you've established it, fleetness of foot and accelerated improvement will come as a result.

Stay Grounded. Show that nothing is beneath you so that others will learn it is not beneath them either. Remember where you came from, and don't hesitate to remind others of their origins as well. Uplifting leaders roll up their sleeves and get involved in the nitty-gritty, irrespective of their role or position. Don't elevate your stars too much, but don't ignore them either. Virtuoso teams consist of passionate, skilled people working under leaders who are not threatened by their strongest players' performance and who are comfortable in their own skin.[12]

Avoid Cliques and Elites. Their secrecy will arouse suspicion among others. Don't forsake the quiet ones for the noisy, sparkly ones when attending organizational gatherings. Be aware of internal rivalries among your own people. Never allow favoritism or nepotism to influence your behavior. Ensure that team loyalty does not undermine excellence or imperil the group's work.

Convert Weakness into Strength. Show genuine humility and acknowledge your own ignorance when appropriate. Admit when you are unsure about what to do, and people will rally round with ideas, suggestions and offers of support. Don't pretend you have all the answers. Use your vulnerabilities to empathize with and advocate for others who struggle or suffer. Make jokes about yourself to endear people to you and make it easier for them to acknowledge their own flaws so that they can seek help as well. When you are struggling, find good listeners who will help you find your way again.

Be aware of both your strongest individuals and your weakest links. Persuade your stars to coach your fledglings. Remember that all participants have value and have to be valued. Penniless supporters can also be priceless volunteers, and everyone can uplift each other.

Conduct Difficult Conversations with Dignity. Dignity is one of the most important things in life. If the struggle for change is too much for some people or beyond their commitments and capabilities, allow people to leave with dignity and with thanks for all they have done. Don't burn bridges or harbor grudges. Take action and move on. Confront inattention or indiscretions before they amplify and spread. When difficult conversations are conducted with dignity in the interests of the individual and also the community, allegiances are ultimately strengthened as even those who leave maintain their respect for you and for themselves.

5. Measuring with Meaning

Measure What You Value—instead of valuing only what you can measure. Demarcate the intermediary steps for reaching your target. Avoid chasing other people's goals that you do not value or respect. But don't be so naïve or dismissive about unwanted metrics that your own survival will become a casualty of them. In reality, if you concentrate on authentically improving your performance, then most of the metrics will take care of themselves. Be the drivers of data; don't be driven *by* them. Use your metrics and monitoring systems to help you know your customers, players, or students, but don't let them become a replacement for those relationships.

Share Your Targets. Raise your own bars, share your own targets, and develop your key performance indicators (KPIs) *together*. Ensure that these targets stretch everyone—including yourself. Ask people to work out ways to measure their own contributions and to bring them to their performance review.

Be Transparent. Rely on real evidence. Don't create smoke and mirrors with false or fancy statistics. Always have your own data and evidence ready to counter negative perceptions and interpretations. Be scrupulously honest; there's no point in fooling yourself. Be as transparent about shortcomings as you are about successes with clients, parents, and fans; these are the people who will help you get back on track.

Interpret Evidence Intelligently. Progress is rarely smooth and continuous, so you must expect that results will fluctuate. Don't be discouraged by a single downturn or unfavorable result; instead, look at the longer-term trends. Do not declare victory too early, either—it may well be just a false recovery. If results take a tumble, don't kill the messenger. Avoid bullwhip reactions and going after scapegoats. Shoulder your share of the blame and sometimes even more than that.

Use data to initiate evidence-based inquiry through constant refinement and checking. Adopt a balanced scorecard. Deliberately seek a wide variety of qualitative and quantitative measures. Don't be dragged on to the rocks by the siren call of the single bottom line. Foster the attitude that it is better to just miss an ambitious target than it is to meet a modest one. Give credit for progress made toward a demanding target, even if the final effort falls slightly short. Regularly review your progress and performance. Focusing exclusively on problems—on performance that is amber or red—won't just depress you; it will also deflect you from seeing what explains your successes. Do pay attention to the reds and ambers, but also make sure that you do not leave your greens.

Make Your Metrics Meaningful. Use proven measurement devices for self-evaluation. Don't be swamped by your own data; you shouldn't spend more time analyzing than on the core tasks that this analysis is supposed to measure. Set goals according to what you want to do next or how you want to be—rather than whom you want to beat or how far you want to go in the long term. Make sure that when you hit your targets, you do not miss the point.

6. Sustainable Success

Grow Your Own Family Tree. Connect yourself back to the foundation that your ancestors built. Acknowledge the work your predecessors did and make it possible for your successors to branch off and grow some more after you have gone. Don't strangle the organization's roots or saw off the branch on which you are sitting. Like the giant redwoods of California, create a strong network of interconnected roots of support that will be the hidden platform for others to grow tall and excel. Always remember that inspiring leaders do not sprout up from nowhere. The people who came before you helped make you what you are.

Appreciate Your Assets. Pause before succumbing to the temptation to sweep aside everyone and everything with a new broom. Clean sweeps often lead only to false recovery or to no recovery at all. Don't just populate the organization by importing people who are already loyal to you; this will alienate all those who carry institutional knowledge and attachment to the organization's existing strengths and traditions. Identify what your existing people have before you begin bemoaning what they lack. Wherever you can, combine external ideas with internal capacities and loyalties in more productive ways.

Grow Sustainably. Invest in the long term. Effective teams and new leaders take many years to develop. Most authentic growth is relentless but steady and sustainable. Like bamboo, only after years of cultivation do sudden spurts in growth begin to show above the surface. Early spikes in results are often fabrications or false recoveries, whereas later spikes are more usually reflective of sustainable investment. Change can come about more quickly after establishing or restoring trust and self-belief. But these things do not themselves come about by instant conversion. Rather, you must bolster them with quick wins that boost confidence. However, you must not make ethical compromises to achieve them or be misled into believing they reflect miraculous changes in core practices and effectiveness.

Grow at a rate you can manage. Avoid burnout by pushing too hard, too fast. Be careful that a pursuit to the top doesn't become a lemming race over a cliff. Acknowledge every fraction of improved performance you gain, no matter how small. As long as you are moving forward you will always have a chance of uplift.

Connect the Dots. An organization or a system is like an impressionist painting or a patchwork quilt: every stitch and stroke matters in the composition of the whole. One key task of uplifting leadership is to connect the various pieces into one comprehensive solution or existence. You must understand and be able to articulate the relationship between where people came from in the past and where they are headed in the future. Show them how a seemingly small piece of work connects to the bigger picture that everyone is creating together. Explain how each tiny step in the short term draws people closer to achieving their long-term dream. Do this not just in occasional speeches, but at every opportunity that presents itself in countless conversations. The points make up the big picture, and the picture justifies every single point. Remember the words that have been attributed to Marco Polo: "Without stones, there is no arch."[13]

Staying Aloft

Though uplifting leaders have inspiring dreams, they are not idle dreamers. They keep their eyes up and their feet always on the ground. They experience fear, like most other mortals, but are not overwhelmed by it. They know how to fight, not in aggressive competition or self-defense, but for a cause that is greater than themselves. They lead from the front when they have to, but lead from behind whenever they can. They can lift and inspire those around them, but also know how to let go and leave it to others. Uplifting leaders have a proper sense of urgency, but they do not deplete their own and others' resources and energy by expanding and changing too fast. They use data and statistics intelligently without being dazzled or driven by them. Uplifting leaders can do a lot with a little, create something from almost nothing, and turn failure into success.

In the end, these uplifting leaders exist not just at the front of their organization, system, or community. We can find them everywhere throughout it—in classrooms, storerooms, and locker rooms; on the bench as well as on the field; behind the throne as well as upon it. Maria Montessori, the inventor of the famed Montessori method of early childhood education, reminded us that a good leader is like a good teacher.[14] And the greatest sign of success for a teacher is to be able to say, "The children are now working as if I did not exist."

This is the ultimate goal of all uplifting leaders. When we eventually step aside and complete our final journey, the good works and the good work should still go on. Our life's work is to help raise others up—our children, our colleagues, and our communities. That becomes our lasting legacy.

Appendix
Research Methodology

The research underpinning this book, and the examples and accounts within it, draw on several interconnected projects that have extended over seven years. They comprise a broader program of work on high performance.[1]

We first came together as researchers to conduct a large-scale international study that during the years 2007–2010 that investigated organizations that *performed beyond expectations* (PBE) in the public and private sectors.[2] This study joined research teams from the United States and the United Kingdom and asked three questions:

- What characteristics make organizations of different types successful and sustainable, far beyond expectations?
- How does sustainability of performance beyond expectations in leadership and change manifest itself in education, compared to other sectors?
- What are the implications for schools and school leaders?

To answer these questions, the research team produced detailed case studies of high-performing organizations in the fields of business, education, and sports. In the sports sector, we studied a large national professional organization (Cricket Australia), local clubs (Burnley Football Club and Hull Kingston Rovers Rugby League Football Club), and one amateur sports organization (Kilkenny Gaelic

Athletic Association). We explored business sector sites within the motor industry (Fiat), global retailing (Marks & Spencer), craft brewery (Dogfish Head Craft Brewery), online footwear (Shoebuy .com), and multinational chemicals (Scott Bader Multinational). To learn about high performance in education, we went to urban local authorities (school districts) and a range of elementary and high schools in England. All our cases met the criteria set for performance beyond expectations that were formed and agreed to by the project team. The research team carefully scrutinized initial data collection before any organization was included in the project to ensure that there were no environmental or ethical concerns. Our standards led us to reject some high-profile potential cases.

The research team conducted two hundred in-depth interviews with leaders and a cross section of respondents through all the eighteen project sites: five in business, four in sports, and nine in English education. A wide range of documentary, contextual, and multimedia evidence supplemented the semistructured interviews. All interviews were transcribed and coded according to a rubric we derived originally from the literature and the interview schedule. The project team deployed within-case and cross-case analysis to elicit themes that were synthesized, revised, and repeatedly tested against the evidence.

We returned all the detailed PBE case studies that extended up to fifteen thousand words to the participating organizations to validate that they were true and accurate accounts, and made changes in response to any concerns about these characteristics. The accounts that appear in this book of all the business cases, and all sports cases except the Vancouver Giants hockey team, plus one of the education cases—Tower Hamlets Local Authority in London—are derived from these much longer and more detailed individual case studies of *performance beyond expectations*. Our initial analysis of these cases appears in the original research report.[3]

In analyzing our original eighteen PBE cases, we developed a framework of fifteen factors, provisionally labeled F factors that explained PBE.[4] Each factor was supported by multiple cases, with at least one example from each of the three sectors investigated. We also cross-analyzed the case studies to test out the F factors and to build explanatory power from comparing the different data sets.

As the project progressed, we began to consider how this particular research project could reach a broader audience. It became clear that we needed an additional North-American-based sport to add to our existing sports sample in cricket, soccer, hurling, and rugby league. We therefore added a site visit to the Vancouver Giants hockey team, and subsequently a case study of the team in 2011. This self-funded addition to our PBE sample used the same methodology, interview protocols, and ethical review procedures as for the cases in the original project.

Another requirement for reaching a wider audience was a more extensive sample of educational cases than those solely based in England (when the geographical parameters of the original sample had been set by our funders). For this reason, we added a further two cases using the same protocols and methods. These cases were the California Teachers' Association that was conducted on a self-funded basis, and the Singapore education system, using funding associated with a visiting professor role at the National Institute of Education in Singapore.[5] Both these additional case studies were conducted in 2011.

For the purposes of this book, we have also drawn from a wider program of our preceding and parallel research work in our shared attention to studying high performance and successful turnarounds. Our discussion of the high-performing education system in Finland draws on a number of sources including Andy Hargreaves' 2007 case study with Beatriz Pont and Gabor Halasz for the Organization for Economic Cooperation and Development (OECD) of leadership patterns in Finland and their relationship to the country's high educational performance.[6]

Our brief discussion of educational reform strategies in Ontario, Canada, draws upon a second research project that Andy Hargreaves and Henry Braun conducted between 2009 and 2012 on the province's systemwide reform initiative in special education, known as Essential for Some, Good for All (ESGA). This project, funded by the Council of Ontario Directors of Education (equivalent to US school superintendents), looked at reform implementation in ten of Ontario's seventy-two school boards. Details of the project's research methodology and findings are available in the final project report.[7]

Last, to complement the London-based study of Tower Hamlets, we also incorporated material from a self-funded study of the work of The Learning Trust in Hackney from 2002 to 2012 by Alan Boyle and Salli Humphreys. The London borough of Hackney achieved a remarkable turnaround in educational performance over one decade. To find out why, the research team interviewed a wide cross-section of thirty-six people who were involved with Hackney education during this period, ranging from the national Secretary of State for Education to frontline staff in the schools. Respondents were asked questions about their involvement with Hackney education; the reasons for Hackney's significant improvements in its examination and test results over the ten-year period; and the role and impact of the private, nonprofit company called The Learning Trust that had been charged with making these improvements.

The team made audio recordings of all conversations that were then coded and analyzed. A triangulation technique—cross-checking multiple sources of data, and multiple perspectives among those who collected or reviewed the data—was used to determine the key issues which crystallized around a genuine consensus about ten characteristics that informed the final set of findings.[8]

As we combined these key elements of the various research programs, we undertook detailed contrast and comparison across the cases. As a result, we condensed our analytical framework from the initial fifteen factors from the original PBE report to the eventual six factors that constitute *Uplifting Leadership*. These six factors form the core chapters of this book. In the final stages of completing the book, we added some new cases that we researched from published secondary sources to provide a more diverse evidence base that illustrates our ideas of uplifting leadership.

Notes

Introduction

1. R. W. Quinn and R. E. Quinn, *Lift: Becoming a Positive Force in Any Situation* (San Francisco: Berrett-Koehler, 2009), 2. When we had analyzed all the data from the cases in our project and induced the overall category and explanation of uplift and uplifting leadership, we could not find any literature on uplifting leadership or uplift in the broad sense that we had discovered, but we did come across Quinn and Quinn's very helpful book, *Lift*. We have undoubtedly gained a great deal from the Quinns' aerodynamic explanation of "lift" and its operation as a social psychological force that is able to "move ourselves and others up to greater heights of achievement, integrity, learning, and love, becoming a positive force in any situation." "When we experience these thoughts and feelings," the Quinns say, "we feel uplifted and lift the people around us," 3. Our own work resonates with the Quinns' social-psychological understanding of lift.

    Our book builds on and adds to their preceding framework in three ways. First, whereas the Quinns draw on the insight of personal experiences, their consulting work with leaders and organizations, and social psychological literature, we have been able to use a detailed database of fifteen high-performing organizations, and to infer the nature and power of uplifting leadership from this evidence base. Second, while Quinn and Quinn's work tends to emphasize the positive psychology aspects of being centered on purposes and personal values, empathy with others, and openness to change, we have also found that there are "hard" as well as "soft" qualities of uplift and uplifting leadership such as grim determination, hard work and struggle, confronting and capitalizing on resistance, working with the dynamics of competition as well as collaboration, and combining the personal knowledge of human relationships with the metrics and navigational tools of hard data. Last, as we will see below, uplift is also historically a sociological force that has underpinned the struggle of minorities such as African Americans and the poor to overcome prejudice, disadvantage, and oppression; it is therefore a force for social justice and the betterment of human life and experience as much as an emotional process of personal improvement and interpersonal influence.

2. In his history of the idea and strategy of uplift among African Americans from the early to mid-nineteenth century, Kevin Gaines describes how "the notion of self-help among blacks as building black homes and promoting family stability came to displace a broader vision of uplift as group struggle for citizenship and material advancement." See K. K. Gaines, *Uplifting the Race: Black Leadership, Politics, and Culture in the Twentieth Century* (Chapel Hill: The University of North Carolina Press, 1996), 6.

3. Retrieved from www.thekingcenter.org/blog/mlk-quote-week-all-labor-uplifts-humanity-has-dignity-and-importance-and-should-be-undertaken.

4. President Obama was accepted into the prestigious Punahou Academy in Hawaii from grade 5 until his graduation in 1979. In his autobiography, Obama writes about the "elevating" effect this had on the family. "For my grandparents, my admission into Punahou Academy heralded the start of something grand, an elevation in the family status that they took great pains to let everyone know." B. Obama, *Dreams from My Father* (New York: Three Rivers Press, 1995), 58.

5. Some of the founding literature in this area of soft skills is more than a quarter century old. For example, Bernard Bass argued that leaders of organizations that perform beyond expectations articulate a convincing and inspiring vision. They appeal to people's emotional engagements and attachments to their leaders and fellow followers so that everyone will be prepared to transform their habits and work practices in order to reach an entirely new level of performance, see B. M. Bass, *Leadership and Performance Beyond Expectations* (New York: Free Press, 1985).

6. Tom Peters' and Bob Waterman's classic study of leading executives in forty-three Fortune 500 companies highlighted the "soft processes" of excellence that explained outstanding performance—including developing people, having clear and common values, and pursuing innovation through effective leadership, see T. J. Peters and R. H. Waterman, *In Search of Excellence: Lessons from America's Best Run Companies* (New York: Grand Central, 1982).

7. J. Collins, *Good to Great: Why Some Companies Make the Leap . . . and Others Don't* (New York: HarperCollins, 2001).

8. R. S. Sisodia, D. B. Wolfe, and J. N. Sheth, *Firms of Endearment: How World-Class Companies Profit from Passion and Purpose* (Upper Saddle River, NJ: Wharton School, 2007), 4.

9. See for example: C. Arena, *Cause for Success: 10 Companies That Put Profits Second and Came in First* (Novato, CA: New World Library, 2004); I. A. Jackson and J. Nelson, *Profits with Principles: Seven Strategies for Delivering Value with Values* (New York: Currency, Doubleday, 2004); B. K. Googins, P. H. Mirvis, and S. A. Rochlin, *Beyond Good Company: Next Generation Corporate Citizenship* (New York: Palgrave Macmillan, 2007); J. Mackey and R. Sisodia, *Conscious Capitalism: Liberating the Heroic Spirit of Business* (Cambridge, MA: Harvard Business Review Press, 2014); N. M. Pless and T. Maak (Eds.), *Responsible Leadership* (Houten, Netherlands: Springer, 2011).

10. For examples of schools that achieve high standards against the odds, see:
    M. Bromberg and C. Theokas, *Breaking the Glass Ceiling of Achievement for Low-Income Students and Students of Color*, Shattering Expectations Series (Washington, DC: The Education Trust, 2013), www .edtrust.org/high_end_gaps.
    R. D. Barr and E. L. Gibson, *Building a Culture of Hope: Enriching Schools with Optimism and Opportunity* (Bloomington, IN: Solution Tree, 2013).
    W. H. Parrett and K. M. Budge, *Turning High-Poverty Schools into High-Performing Schools* (Alexandria, VA: ASCD, 2012).
    I. Siraj-Blatchford, "Learning in the Home and at School: How Working-Class Children 'Succeed Against the Odds,'" *British Educational Research Journal* 36, No. 3 (2010): 463–482.
    K. Chenoweth, *How It's Being Done: Urgent Lessons from Unexpected Schools* (Cambridge, MA: Harvard Education Press, 2009).

11. M. Fullan and A. Boyle, *Big-City School Reforms: Lessons from New York, Toronto and London* (New York: Teachers College Press, 2014).

12. Peters and Waterman, *In Search of Excellence.*

13. J. Collins, *How the Mighty Fall* (New York: HarperCollins, 2009).

14. A. Hargreaves and D. Shirley, *The Global Fourth Way: The Quest for Educational Excellence* (Thousand Oaks, CA: Corwin, 2012).

15. A. Rappaport, "The Economics of Short-Term Performance Obsession," *Financial Analysts Journal* 61, No. 3 (2005): 65. Also see K. J. Laverty, "Managerial Myopia or Systemic Short-Termism?: The Importance of Managerial Systems in Valuing the Long Term," *Management Decision* 42, No. 8 (2004): 949–962.

16. E. P. Lazear, "Speeding, Terrorism and Teaching to the Test," *The Quarterly Journal of Economics* 121, No. 3 (2006): 1029–1061. A. Hargreaves and H. Braun, *Data Driven Improvement and Accountability* (Boulder, CO: National Education Policy Center, 2013).

17. The current US educational reform strategy is actually called Race to the Top. One of the most vocal of its critics is Diane Ravitch; see D. Ravitch, *Reign of Error: The Hoax of the Privatization Movement and the Danger to America's Public Schools* (New York: Knopf, 2013).

18. For a view of inspirational leadership grounded in myth and drama see R. Olivier, *Inspirational Leadership: Timeless Lessons for Leaders from Shakespeare's Henry V* (Boston: Nicholas Brealey, 2013). For a more traditionally academic view see B. M. Bass, "The Inspirational Processes of Leadership," *Journal of Management Development* 7, No. 5 (1988): 21–31.

    For a scholarly view of transformational leadership see B. M. Bass and R. E. Riggio, *Transformational Leadership* (Mahwah, NJ: Erlbaum, 2006). For a practical perspective from a turnaround business leader see R. Dobbs, with P. R. Walker, *Transformational Leadership: A Blueprint for Real Organizational Change* (Marion, MI: Parkhurst Brothers, 2010). And for an educational perspective see K. Leithwood, D. Jantzi, and R. Steinbach, *Changing Leadership for Changing Times* (Florence, KY: Taylor & Francis, 1999).

Chapter 1

1. Retrieved from www.thekingcenter.org/archive/document/i-have-dream-1.

2. Retrieved from http://corporate.ford.com/news-center/press-releases-detail/pr-opening-the-highways-artwork-38208.

3. P. Betts and M. Nakamoto, "Fiat Boldly Goes Where Others Fear to Tread," *Financial Times*, January 20, 2009.

4. J. Trop, "Fiat, in Deal with Union, Will Buy Rest of Chrysler," *New York Times*, January 1, 2014, www.nytimes.com/2014/01/02/business/fiat-in-deal-with-union-will-buy-rest-of-chrysler.html?_r=0; The Economist, "Hoping It Will Hold Together," *The Economist*, August 24, 2013, www.economist.com/news/business/21584001-union-fiat-and-chrysler-has-better-chances-both-carmakers-previous-alliancesbut.

5. E. Sylvers, "In Helping Chrysler, Fiat May Find an Opportunity," *New York Times*, March 31, 2009, www.nytimes.com/2009/04/01/business/01fiat.html?_r=1&. Our team conducted a three-day site visit to Fiat Auto, in Turin, in January 2009. Shortly afterward, at a time of ensuing restructurings and staff reallocations accompanying the

alliance and partnership with Chrysler, the executives with whom we had been working most closely, and who facilitated our visit, left the company for other positions. These staff changes made it difficult to complete the ethical review process and make use of firsthand data. However, the manifestly uplifting example that Fiat represented led us to collect, analyze, and report on a wealth of secondary public domain data from websites, news and magazine articles, speeches and reports, and scholarly articles. The particular sources are listed in the endnotes that follow.

6. C. Whitlock and S. Mufson, "Once-Struggling Fiat Could Become No. 3 World Automaker with GM, Chrysler Deals," *Washington Post*, May 17, 2009, www.washingtonpost.com/wp-dyn/content/article/2009/05/16/AR2009051602319.html.

7. C. Castelli, M. Florio, and A. Giunta, "The Competitive Repositioning of the Automotive District of Turin: Innovation, Internationalisation and the Role of ICT," Milan University, May 6, 2008.

8. "Reborn Fiat Shakes Up Italian Stereotype," *The Economic Times International*, May 11, 2009, articles.economictimes.indiatimes.com/2009–05–11/news/27655883_1_italian-automaker-fiat-brand-sergio-marchionne.

9. S. Marchionne, Speech by the Chief Executive of Fiat: Sergio Marchionne, Conferment of honorary degree in industrial engineering and management, Politecnico Di Torino, May 27, 2008, 26. Download pdf at https://www.fiatgroup.com/en-us/joinfiat/Documents/lectio_marchionne_eng.pdf.

10. Whitlock and Mufson, "Once-Struggling Fiat."

11. S. Marchionne, "Fiat's Extreme Makeover," *Harvard Business Review*, December, 2008, 45, hbr.org/2008/12/fiats-extreme-makeover/ar/1.

12. La Repubblica's US correspondent Vittorio Zucconi is quoted in *Reborn Fiat*, 2009.

13. N. Bunkley, "U.S. to Sell Its Chrysler Stake to Fiat," *New York Times*, June 2, 2011, www.nytimes.com/2011/06/03/business/03auto.html?_r=0.

14. See E. Reguly, "A Green Method Spurs Fiat's Madness," *The Globe and Mail*, May 11, 2009, www.theglobeandmail.com/report-on-business/rob-commentary/a-green-method-spurs-fiats-madness/article784786/; the quotation is from The Economist, "Saving Fiat: Sergio Marchionne Thinks He Can Salvage Italy's Flagship Company," *The Economist*, December 1, 2005, www.economist.com/node/5263417?zid=293&ah=e50f636873b42369614615ba3c16df4a.

15. The Economist, "Hoping It Will Hold Together."

16. Marchionne, "Fiat's Extreme Makeover."

17. S. Pattuglia, *Integrated Marketing Communication and Brand Management: the Case Study of Fiat 500*. DSI Essay Series, No. 18. (Milano: McGraw-Hill, 2011), 18.

18. C. Gilson, M. Pratt, K. Roberts, and E. Weymes, *Peak Performance: Business Lessons from the World's Top Sports Organizations* (London, England: Harper Collins, 2001), 29. This collection of twelve cases of peak-performing sports teams from across the world by New Zealand authors Gilson and colleagues is one of the few and certainly the most significant cross-case analyses of high performance in the sports sector and the organizational reasons underpinning it.

19. G. Erikson and L. Lorentzen, *Raising the Bar: Integrity and Passion in Life and Business: The Story of Clif Bar Inc.* (San Francisco: Jossey-Bass, 2004), 252.

20. Clif Bar, *Raising the Bar: All Aspirations Annual Report*, Berkeley, CA, Clif Bar & Co., 2009.

21. Erikson and Lorentzen, 253.

22. J. L. Badaracco, *The Good Struggle: Responsible Leadership in an Unforgiving World* (Cambridge, MA: Harvard Business Press, 2013).

23. See S. Spencer, "Biggest Patent Goof in History?" May 7, 2009, blog.stevenspencer.net/2009/05/17/biggest-patent-goof-in-history/.

24. The NAEP Data Explorer makes it possible to create statistical tables, charts and maps in order to explore decades of assessments of students' achievements and analyze them state by state. Data retrieved from nces.ed.gov/nationsreportcard/naepdata/.
The figures for 2003 are cited in S. J. Caroll, C. Krop, J. Arkes, P. A. Morrison, and A. Flanagan, *California's K–12 Public Schools: How Are They Doing?* (Santa Monica, CA: RAND, 2005), xxxiv.

25. Unless otherwise stated, all data, quotations and information on this and the following pages about the work of the CTA to implement the QEIA were collected from primary sources during case study research carried out by Andy Hargreaves and Dennis Shirley within the broader protocols and frameworks of the overall study. See Appendix.

26. California Department of Education, *Report to the Legislature and the Governor: Quality Education Investment Act*, First Progress Report, January 2010, www.cde.ca.gov/ta/lp/qe/.

27. C. L. Malloy and A. K. Nee, *Lessons from the Classroom: Initial Success for At-Risk Students, A Report on the Quality Education Investment Act* (Los Angeles: Vital Research, 2010).

28. T. M. Moe, *Special Interest: Teacher Unions and America's Public Schools* (Washington, DC: The Brookings Institution, 2011).

29. P. Brimelow, *The Worm in the Apple: How the Teacher Unions Are Destroying American Education* (New York: Perennial, HarperCollins, 2003).

30. See note #26, 2010.

31. A. Smarick, "The Turnaround Fallacy," *Education Next* 10 No. 1 (2010): 20–26. See also H. Mintrop, "The Limits of Sanctions in Low Performing Schools, a Study of Maryland and Kentucky Schools on Probation," *Education Policy Analysis Archives*, 11, No. 3 (2003), epaa.asu.edu/ojs/article/view/231.

C. Payne, *So Much Reform, So Little Change: The Persistence of Failure in Urban Schools* (Cambridge, MA: Harvard Education Press, 2010).

A. Daly, "Rigid Response in an Age of Accountability: The Potential of Leadership and Trust," in *Educational Administration Quarterly* 45, No. 2 (2009):168–216.

32. Quoted in C. L. Malloy and A. K. Nee, *Cultivating Change in Schools: A Deeper Look at QEIA Implementation* (Los Angeles: Vital Research, 2013): 15.

33. S. Snyder, *Leadership and the Art of Struggle: How Great Leaders Grow through Challenge and Adversity* (San Francisco: Berrett-Koehler, 2013).

34. J. M. Fenster, "The Woman Who Invented the Dishwasher," *American Heritage of Invention & Technology*, Fall 1999: 59, http://50.57.231.74/IT/content/woman-who-invented-dishwasher-1?page=3.

35. S. Marchionne, Speech by the Chief Executive of Fiat: Sergio Marchionne.

36. E. Reguly, "Transatlantic Man," *Globe and Mail Report on Business*, December 2009: 40.

37. For a contemporary view of one of Churchill's many famous quotations, see G. Loftus, "'If You're Going Through Hell Keep Going'—Churchill," *Forbes*, May 9, 2012, www.forbes.com/sites/geoffloftus/2012/05/09/if-youre-going-through-hell-keep-going-winston-churchill/.

38. "DuPont CEO Ellen Kullman's Four Principles for Moving Ahead during Turbulent Times," *Knowledge@Wharton*, E. Kullman, speaking at 13th Annual Wharton Leadership Conference, June 24, 2009, knowledge.wharton.upenn.edu/article/dupont-ceo-ellen-kullmans-four-principles-for-moving-ahead-during-turbulent-times/.

39. "Ellen Kullman, DuPont CEO: Women in Leadership," *NBR*, September 16, 2011, wp.nbr.com/women_in_leadership/ ellen-kullman-dupont-ceo-women-in-leadership-20110916.

40. "The Science of Success: DuPont's Ellen Kullman," *EY*, 2012, www .ey.com/US/en/Services/Strategic-Growth-Markets/Exceptional-January-June-2012—-The-science-of-success—-DuPonts-Ellen-Kullman.

41. M. S. Whittle, "DuPont CEO Ellen Kullman Discusses Market-Driven Science, Finding Sustainable Solutions to Global Challenges," *UVA Today*, April 2, 2013, news.virginia.edu/content/dupont-ceo-ellen-kull-man-discusses-market-driven-science-finding-sustainable-solutions.

42. R. Kirkland, "Leading in the 21st Century: An Interview with Ellen Kullman," *McKinsey & Co.*, September 2012, www.mckinsey.com/ insights/leading_in_the_21st_century/an_interview_with_ellen_kullman.

43. "Interview with Ellen Kullman, Chair of the Board and CEO DuPont," *ISO*, March 28, 2013, www.iso.org/iso/news.htm?refid=Ref1724.

44. For more information about the Global Collaboratory and the partnership with Repshel, see "Helping to Build Affordable Homes in Campeche," www.dupont.com/corporate-functions/our-approach/global-challenges/ protection/articles/affordable-homes.html.

45. For DuPont's record on pollution see GM Watch, www.gmwatch.org/ latest-listing/1-news-items/7987-dupont-one-of-the-worlds-worst-polluters-2912002. For DuPont's recent awards, see PR Web, www .prweb.com/releases/dupont_sustainability/corporate_responsibility/ prweb10627177.htm.

46. "DuPont CEO Ellen Kullman's Four Principles." See note 38.

47. "The Science of Success: DuPont's Ellen Kullman," *EY*, 2012, www .ey.com/US/en/Services/Strategic-Growth-Markets/Exceptional-January-June-2012—-The-science-of-success—-DuPonts-Ellen-Kullman.

48. Extracted from a conversation with Ellen Kullman at The Economic Club, October 10, 2013 www.economicclub.org/doc_repo/Kullman%20 Transcript.pdf.

49. "Ellen Kullman, DuPont CEO: Women in Leadership," *NBR*, September 16, 2011, wp.nbr.com/women_in_leadership/ ellen-kullman-dupont-ceo-women-in-leadership-20110916.

50. Unless otherwise stated, all data, quotations, and information about Burnley Football Club on this and the following pages were collected from primary sources during the Performance Beyond Expectations research. See Appendix.

51. The English indices of deprivation identify the most deprived areas across the country. They combine data from a range of indicators covering

economic, social, and housing issues. The 326 local authority districts are ranked in terms of deprivation. They are used to identify areas that would benefit from special government initiatives and they determine eligibility for various programs that carry additional funding. The index of deprivation is discussed at www.theguardian.com/news/datablog/2011/mar/29/indices-multiple-deprivation-poverty-england. In 2010, Burnley District ranked twenty-first out of 326 districts in terms of overall deprivation, see *English Indices of Deprivation 2010: Local Authority Summaries*, www.gov.uk/government/publications/english-indices-of-deprivation-2010.

52. The quotation is from Campbell's review on November 9, 2012, of the book *Magical: A Life in Football* by former Chief Executive Paul Fletcher and Dave Thomas (Skipton, UK: Vertical Editions, 2012). The review can be downloaded from http://www.thefootballnetwork.net/main/s37/st179882.htm?print=1.

53. These quotations on the financial crisis are from former Chairman Barry Kilby.

54. This quotation on Coyle's character is from former Operational Director Brendan Flood.

55. These are quotations from Wade Elliott, one of Burnley's leading players under Coyle's management. See Geldard, S., "Owen Coyle's 2nd Anniversary at Burnley: Gaffer Lets Us Express Ourselves, Says Elliott," *Lancashire Evening Telegraph*, November 18, 2009, www.lancashiretelegraph.co.uk/sport/4741157.Owen_Coyle_s_2nd_anniversary_at_Burnley__Gaffer_lets_us_express_ourselves__says_Elliott/.

56. S. Geldard, "I Owe Dyche So Much, Says Burnley Winger," *Lancashire Telegraph*, January 18, 2014, www.lancashiretelegraph.co.uk/sport/football/burnley_fc/news/10946616.I_owe_Dyche_so_much__says_Burnley_winger/.

Chapter 2

1. Many books of Frost's collected works contain this classic. See, for example, R. Frost, *The Road Not Taken and Other Poems* (Mineola: Dover Thrift Editions, 1993).

2. I. Arreguín-Toft, *How the Weak Win Wars: A Theory of Asymmetric Conflict* (Cambridge, UK: Cambridge University Press, 2005).

3. K. Robinson, *The Element: How Finding Your Passion Changes Everything* (New York: Penguin, 2009), 21.

4. See the interview with Frank Nuovo, formerly of Nokia, in The *Financial Review*. P. Smith, "The Nokia Insider Who Knows

Why It Failed Warns Apple It Could Be Next," *Financial Review*, September 6, 2013, www.afr.com/p/technology/ next_nokia_insider_who_knows_why_Z8at1lqZLp3mAutUOOye0H.

5. See J. Michelli, *The Starbucks Experience: 5 Principles for Turning Around the Ordinary into the Extraordinary* (New York: McGraw-Hill, 2007).

6. See P. Howard and G. Ogilvie, *Concentration in the U.S. Beer Industry*, 2011, www.msu.edu/~howardp/beer.html.

7. Unless otherwise indicated, all data, quotations and information about Dogfish Head Craft Brewery on this and the following pages were collected from primary sources during the Performance Beyond Expectations research. See Appendix.

8. Comparative statistics on production, market share, and other relevant indicators have been drawn from Brewers Association, *Craft Brewing Statistics*, 2009. Accessed August 17, 2009, at www.beertown.org/ craftbrewing/statistics.html and IBISWorld (2009), *Beer Production: U.S. Industry Report*. Available online at www.ibisworld.com.

9. See B. Bilger, "A Better Brew: The Rise of Extreme Beer," *The New Yorker*, November 24, 2008, www.newyorker.com/reporting/2008/11/24/ 081124fa_fact_bilger.

   For books by Sam Calagione, see S. Calagione, *Extreme Brewing: An Introduction to Brewing Craft Beer at Home* (Beverly, MA: Quarry Books, 2012), and Calagione, S., *Brewing Up a Business: Adventures in Beer from the Founder of Dogfish Head Craft Brewery* (Hoboken, NJ: Wiley, 2011).

10. J. Collins and M. T. Hansen, *Great by Choice* (New York: Harper Business, 2011).

11. Collins and Hansen, 78.

12. See C. Salter, "Failure Doesn't Suck," *Fast Company*, May 2007, www .fastcompany.com/59549/failure-doesnt-suck.

13. "Failure Doesn't Suck."

14. T. Kelley and D. Kelley, *Creative Confidence: Unleashing the Creative Potential Within Us All* (New York: Crown Publishing, 2013), p 51. This approach to failure is what John Maxwell calls "failing forward," see J. Maxwell, *Failing Forward: Turning Mistakes into Stepping Stones for Success* (Nashville: Thomas Nelson, 2007).

15. "Video Killed the Radio Star," written by Trevor Horn, Geoff Downes, and Bruce Woolley, 1978. Recorded by The Buggles in 1979 on Island Records.

16. Retrieved from www.forbes.com/sites/erikaandersen/2013/05/31/21-quotes-from-henry-ford-on-business-leadership-and-life/.

17. One of the best-known exponents of this idea is Peter Senge in his view of organizational learning. See P. Senge, *The Fifth Discipline: The Art and Practice of the Learning Organization* (New York: Doubleday, 1990).

18. See the transcript of Anna Warman's interview with Sir David Attenborough about his journey to Singapore in 1954, www.warman .demon.co.uk/anna/att_int.html.

19. Unless otherwise stated, all data, quotations and information on this and the following pages about the Singapore education system were collected from primary sources during research carried out in connection with our program on high performance by Andy Hargreaves and Professor Pak Tee Ng of the National Institute of Education (NIE) in Singapore. The work was conducted with the support of the NIE while Andy Hargreaves served as the Visiting C. J. Koh Professor during 2011. See Appendix.

20. In terms of population, Singapore is similar in size to Colorado or Minnesota; however, Singapore is geographically much smaller than these states and its population density is much closer to that in parts of Los Angeles and New York City. Population statistics for Singapore retrieved from www.singstat.gov.sg/statistics/latest_data.html#14; for the United States retrieved from www.census.gov/.

21. Singapore's GDP per capita is fifth in the world, see Index Mundi, *Country Comparison: GDP per Capita*, 2011, www.indexmundi.com/g/r. aspx?t+10&v+67&1=en;.

22. The Singapore GDP annual growth rate peaked at almost 20 percent during 2010, maintaining roughly 15 percent overall. See "Trading Economics," www.tradingeconomics.com/singapore/gdp-growth-annual.

23. Singapore was the top performing country in the 2012 PISA results. It was second to Shanghai overall, which was the top jurisdiction. PISA results were retrieved from www.oecd.org/pisa/keyfindings/pisa-2012-results.htm.

24. The best known example is the Trends in International Mathematics and Science Study (TIMMS) where Singapore was again in the top two performers in 2012. See www.moe.gov.sg/media/press/2012/12/international-studies-affirm-s.php.

25. One school in Singapore, the Anglo Chinese School, obtained thirty-two perfect scores, making up almost half of the candidates worldwide who achieved a perfect score of 45; see www.straitstimes.com/breaking-news/singapore/story/singapore-comes-out-tops-the-fourth-year-international-baccalaureate-e and www.straitstimes.com/breaking-news/singapore/story/32-acs-i-students-attain-perfect-scores-ib-exam-20140106.

Further information about the international baccalaureate is available from www.ibo.org/facts/statbulletin/dpstats/index.cfm.

26. For wider policy overviews of Singapore's economic and educational performance and development, see

M. Mourshed, C. Chijioke, and M. Barber, *How the World's Most Improved School Systems Keep Getting Better.* (London: McKinsey, 2010).

OECD. *Lessons from PISA for the United States, Strong Performers and Successful Reformers in Education* (OECD Publishing, 2011), doi: dx.doi.org/10.1787/9789264096660-en.

M. S. Tucker, *Standing on the Shoulders of Giants: An American Agenda for Education Reform* (Washington, DC: National Center on Education and the Economy, 2011).

27. One of America's leading writers on the paradoxical educational trends in the United States and Asia is Y. Zhao, *Catching Up or Leading the Way? American Education in the Age of Globalization* (Alexandria, VA: Association for Supervision and Curriculum Development, 2009).

28. See "Ten Years On: How Asia Shrugged Off Its Economic Crisis," *The Economist*, July 4, 2007, www.economist.com/node/9432495.

29. C. T. Goh, *Shaping Our Future: Thinking Schools, Learning Nation.* Speech by Prime Minister Goh Chok Tong at the opening of the 7th international conference on thinking on Monday, June 2, 1997 at the Suntec City Convention Centre Ballroom, Singapore. Retrieved September 25, 2011, from www.moe.gov.sg/media/speeches/1997/020697.htm.

30. Ministry of Education, Singapore, *Teach Less, Learn More*, 2005. Retrieved April 20, 2009, from www3.moe.edu.sg/bluesky/print_tllm.htm.

31. H. L. Lee, "Our Future of Opportunity and Promise." Singapore Government Press Release. Address by Prime Minister Lee Hsien Loong at the 2004 National Day Rally, Singapore, August 2004.

32. Ministry of Education, *Teach Less, Learn More*.

33. A. Ahrendts, "Burberry's CEO on Turning an Aging British Icon into a Global Luxury Brand," *Harvard Business Review* (January-February, 2013), hbr.org/2013/01/burberrys-ceo-on-turning-an-aging-british-icon-into-a-global-luxury-brand/ar/1.

34. The Burberry heritage is described in full on the company website, see uk.burberry.com/heritage/#/heritage/heritage-1800–1.

35. J. Geoghegan, "Customer Service and Technological Focus Power Burberry's Success Story," *Drapers Online*, January 16, 2014, www.drapersonline.com/news/customer-service-and-technological-focus-power-burberrys-success-story/5056604.article?blocktitle=More-Fashion-News&contentID=7468.

36. Ahrendts, "Turning an Aging British Icon."

37. Ibid.

38. Ibid.

39. D. Arthurs, "Burberry Hits 10 Million Mark to Become Most Popular Luxury Brand on Facebook," *Daily Mail*, January 4, 2012, www.dailymail. co.uk/femail/article-2082075/Burberry-hits-10m-mark-popular-luxury-brand-Facebook.html.

40. A. Stone, "Burberry Checked over Move to China," *The Independent*, January 7, 2007, www.independent.co.uk/news/business/news/burberry-checked-over-move-to-china-430490.html.

41. S. Butler, J. Rankin, and J. Garside, "Angela Ahrendts Leaves Burberry for New Job at Apple," *The Guardian*, October 15, 2013, www.theguardian. com/business/2013/oct/15/burberry-angela-ahrendts-new-job-apple.

Chapter 3

1. See D. C. McClelland, J. W. Atkinson, R. A. Clark, E. L. Lowell, *The Achievement Motive* (San Francisco: Wiley, 1976); also D. C. McClelland, *Motives, Personality and Society* (New York: Praeger, 1984). McClelland went on to found McBer and Associates, which became part of the global consulting firm Hay Group and Associates in the 1980s.

2. J. Mackey and R. Sisodia, *Conscious Capitalism: Liberating the Heroic Spirit of Business* (Cambridge, MA: Harvard Business Review Press, 2014).

3. Ibid., 90.

4. Ibid., 92.

5. On the evolutionary stages of Corporate Social Responsibility see W. Visser, *The Age of Responsibility: CSR 2.0 and the New DNA of Business* (San Francisco: Wiley, 2011). The extension of these ideas to the concept of corporate citizenship is discussed in B. Googins, P. H. Mirvis, and S. A. Rochlin, *Beyond Good Company: Next Generation of Corporate Citizenship* (Basingstoke, England: Palgrave MacMillan, 2007). See also S. Waddock and A. Rasche, *Building the Responsible Enterprise: Where Vision and Values Add Value* (Redwood City, CA: Stanford University Press, 2012).

6. This quotation is widely cited. It is even possible to purchase a mug online inscribed with the quotation.

7. At the time of data collection for this study, in early 2009, Australia ranked Number 1 in men's international test cricket and second in one-day cricket. At the time of going to press in early 2014, after a 5–0 series victory over England, Australia moved back up to third place after a dip in performance.

International cricket rankings can be accessed on the website of the International Cricket Council at www.icc-cricket.com/team-rankings/test.

8. Unless otherwise stated, all data, quotations, and information about Cricket Australia on this and the following pages were collected from primary sources during the Performance Beyond Expectations research. See Appendix.

9. Markham has changed jobs more than once since the completion of our study. At the time of going to press, he was vice president, Media Distribution for Europe, Middle East, and Africa for the National Basketball Association (NBA).

10. This quotation comes from an interview with a former member of Cricket Australia's leadership team.

11. See A. M. Brandenburger and B. J. Nalebuff, *Co-opetition*, (New York: Bantam Doubleday Dell, 1996).

12. Economist Intelligence Unit, *Companies without Borders: Collaborating to Compete*, 2006, accessed at ilo.uniroma3.it/NEWSILO/vdoc/ Approfondimenti/eiu_BT_collaboration_wp.pdf.

13. A. Slywotzky and C. Hoban, "Stop Competing Yourself to Death: Strategic Collaboration among Rivals," *Journal of Business Strategy*, 28, No. 3 (2007): 45–55.

14. A. Saxenian, *Regional Advantage: Culture and Competition in Silicon Valley and Route 128* (Cambridge, MA: Harvard University Press, 1996).

15. E. Reguly, "Transatlantic Man," *Globe and Mail Report on Business*, December 2009, 44.

16. See R. M. Kanter, "Collaborative Advantage: The Art of Alliances," *Harvard Business Review*, 72, No. 4 (July–August 1994): 96–108. For one of the earliest discussions about the opportunities and risks of combining collaboration and competition, see G. Hamel, Y. L. Doz, and C. K. Prahalad, "Collaborate with Your Competitors—And Win," *Harvard Business Review*, 67, No. 1 (1989): 133–139, hbr.org/1989/01/ collaborate-with-your-competitors-and-win/ar/1.

17. See M. Old and S. Calagione, *He Said Beer, She Said Wine* (New York: Dorling Kindersley, 2008).

18. In 2010 Hackney was the most deprived local authority in England. See *English Indices of Deprivation 2010: Local Authority Summaries*, www.gov. uk/government/publications/english-indices-of-deprivation-2010.

19. A full account of the struggle to close Hackney Downs School is in M. Barber, *The Learning Game* (London: Victor Gollancz, 1996).

20. Audit Commission, November 2000, *Hackney LBC Corporate Governance Inspection*, archive.audit-commission.gov.uk/auditcommission/

inspection-assessment/local-gov-inspection/reports/pages/corporategovernance_15.aspx.html.

21. P. Barker, "Hackney Council a Load of Rubbish," *London Evening Standard*, November 9, 2000.

22. D. Walker and R. Smithers, "Borough of Hate and Hit Squads," *The Guardian*, March 19, 1999, www.theguardian.com/politics/1999/mar/19/uk.politicalnews3.

23. BBC News, "Nord Anglia to Run Hackney School Services," *BBC News*, June 18, 1999, news.bbc.co.uk/1/hi/education/372575.stm.

24. All data, quotations and information about the work of The Learning Trust in Hackney on this page and those following were collected from primary sources during extended research over its ten-year contract. See A. Boyle and S. Humphreys, *A Revolution in a Decade* (London: Leannta, 2012).

25. Academies are publicly funded schools outside the local authority (school district) system. They have more freedom over staffing, the curriculum, and the length of the school day. They are sponsored by a foundation, business, charity, faith group, or university. They receive extra funding from the government compared to their neighboring schools in the local authority.

26. St. John & St. James is a single school. Before its turnaround, it was a failing school with a different name.

27. England's external inspection body for schools is known as OFSTED—an acronym for the Office for Standards in Education. OFSTED inspections judge schools on a 4-point scale: Outstanding; Good; Requires Improvement; Inadequate (Failing school). When a school is judged "Inadequate" the local authority may intervene and either close it or help to improve it by using "special measures."

28. The idea of distributed leadership is increasingly important in education but often misunderstood as delegation, or handing out routine, less important or unwanted tasks to other people. For deeper discussions of distributed leadership, see: A. Harris, *Distributed Leadership Matters* (Thousand Oaks, CA: Corwin, 2013) and J. P. Spillane, *Distributed Leadership* (San Francisco: Jossey-Bass, 2006).

29. Further information about the Primary Advantage Federation in Hackney is available on the federation website: primaryadvantage.co.uk/about/.

30. C. Chapman, D. Muijs, and J. MacAllister, *A Study of the Impact of School Federation on Student Outcomes* (Nottingham, UK: National College for School Leadership, 2011).

31. For a development of this argument see A. Hargreaves and D. Shirley, *The Global Fourth Way* (Thousand Oaks, CA: Corwin Press, 2012), 31–32.

32. Much of the material that follows is taken from J. Steel, M. Wilcox, and M. Hill, "Exploring System-Wide Change: The Academies of Nashville," in *Sustainable School Transformation: An Inside-Out School-Led Approach*, ed. D. Crossley (London: Bloomsbury Academic, 2013), 127–157.

33. Steel, et al., 147.

34. This evaluation is reported in A. Hargreaves, D. Shirley, M. Evans, C. Johnson, and D. Riseman, *The Long and Short of School Improvement: Final Evaluation of the Raising Achievement Transforming Learning Programme of the Specialist Schools and Academies Trust* (London: Specialist Schools and Academies Trust, 2007).

35. The details in this paragraph come from a personal communication from Crossley on December 1, 2013.

36. S. K. Heng, "Our Children. Our Purpose. Our Future." Speech presented by Mr. Heng Swee Keat, Minister for Education, at the Ministry of Education (MOE) Work Plan Seminar 2011 at the Ngee Ann Polytechnic Convention Centre on Thursday, September 22, 2011. Retrieved September 23, 2011, from www.moe.gov.sg/media/speeches/2011/09/22/ work-plan-seminar-2011.php.

37. The parable of the talents (or bags of gold) appears in Matthew's gospel, 25:14–30.

38. M. S. Whittle, "DuPont CEO Ellen Kullman Discusses Market-Driven Science, Finding Sustainable Solutions to Global Challenges," *UVA Today*, April 2, 2013, news.virginia.edu/content/dupont-ceo-ellen-kull-man-discusses-market-driven-science-finding-sustainable-solutions.

39. For more information about the environmental benefits of bio-derived deicers see www.dupont.com/corporate-functions/our-approach/global-challenges/protection/articles/environmentally-sustainable-deicing-fluid.html.

40. The environmental benefits of biobutanol are explained in this short video www.youtube.com/watch?v=K4SKsv4jws8.

41. Extracted from a conversation with Ellen Kullman at The Economic Club, October 10, 2013, www.economicclub.org/doc_repo/Kullman%20 Transcript.pdf.

42. M. Hiltzik, "Cable Monopolies Hurt Consumers and the Nation," *Los Angeles Times*, August 23, 2013, articles.latimes.com/2013/aug/23/busi-ness/la-fi-hiltzik-20130823. See also S. P. Crawford, *Captive Audience: The Telecom Industry and Monopoly Power in the New Gilded Age* (New Haven, CT: Yale University Press, 2013).

43. See S. Baddeley and K. James, "Owl, Fox, Donkey, or Sheep: Political Skills for Managers," *Management Education and Development* 18, No. 1 (1987): 3–19.

Chapter 4

1. A. Dumas, *The Three Musketeers* (New York: Bantam Books, 1984). Originally published 1844.
2. D. McGregor, *The Human Side of Enterprise* (New York: McGraw-Hill, 1960).
3. The story of Marks & Spencer is introduced in full in chapter 6. This item of information came from an article by Sir Stuart Rose on the changing role of business leaders in *The Guardian*, March 29, 2012, www.theguardian.com/sustainable-business/ sir-stuart-rose-changing-role-business-leaders.
4. We learn more about Shoebuy.com in chapter 5.
5. All data, quotations and information about Scott Bader on this and the following pages were collected from primary sources during the Performance Beyond Expectations research, see Appendix. This primary data was supplemented by information from the company website www .scottbader.com/. For historical information and background about Ernest Bader, the founder of Scott Bader Commonwealth, see S. Hoe, *The Man Who Gave His Company Away* (London: Heinemann, 1978).
6. J. Hegel III, J. S. Brown, and L. Davidson, *The Power of Pull: How Small Moves, Smartly Made, Can Set Things in Motion* (New York: Basic Books, 2010).
7. This quotation was from a senior executive.
8. Merriam-Webster dictionary, www.merriam-webster.com/dictionary/ team.
9. All data, quotations and information about Kilkenny hurling on this page and the following pages were collected from primary sources during the Performance Beyond Expectations research, see Appendix.
10. This pushing and pulling dynamic is the essence of strong teams, or what Andy Boynton and Bill Fischer call *virtuoso teams*—teams of extraordinary people with large egos who galvanize together to address tasks like the Manhattan Project that are greater than any of them. See A. Boynton and B. Fisher, *Virtuoso Teams: Lessons from Teams That Changed Their Worlds*, New York: Prentice Hall, 2005). There is vast literature on teams and teaming and their implications for leadership. For a view of how this work

applies to senior teams, especially, read R. Wageman, D. A. Nunes,
J. A. Burruss, and J. R. Hackman, *Senior Leadership Teams: What It Takes
to Make Them Great.* (Cambridge, MA: Harvard Business School Press,
2008).

11. For a history of Huguenot immigration to London's East End, see
www.oldbaileyonline.org/static/Huguenot.jsp. For Jewish immigration,
see www.bbc.co.uk/legacies/immig_emig/england/london/article_2.
shtml.

12. All data, quotations, and information about Tower Hamlets on this page
and the following pages were collected from primary sources during the
Performance Beyond Expectations research, see Appendix.

13. In 2010 Tower Hamlets was the third most deprived local authority in England. With Hackney the most deprived, London's East
End covers a wide area of deprivation. The deprivation indicators we have used for Tower Hamlets are the same as the indicators
for Hackney and Burnley. See *English Indices of Deprivation 2010:
Local Authority Summaries*, www.gov.uk/government/publications/
english-indices-of-deprivation-2010.

14. For an interactive map of the murder locations, see www.casebook.org/
victims/map.html.

15. For criticisms of these simplistic and ineffective punishment-reward
mechanisms in school reform, see for example J. Mehta, *The Allure
of Order: High Hopes, Dashed Expectations and the Troubled Quest to
Remake American Schooling* (New York: Oxford University Press, 2013);
A. Hargreaves and M. Fullan, *Professional Capital: Transforming
Teaching in Every School* (New York: Teachers College Press, 2012);
and D. Ravitch, *Reign of Error: The Hoax of the Privatization
Movement and the Danger to America's Public Schools* (New York: Knopf,
2013).

16. The merit pay initiative was evaluated by the RAND corporation and
then abandoned after the report was published; see J. A. Marsh, M. G.
Springer, D. F. McCaffrey, K. Yuan, S. Epstein, J. Koppich, N. Kalra, C.
DiMartino, and A. (Xiao) Peng, *A Big Apple for Educators: New York
City's Experiment With School-Wide Performance Bonuses* (Santa Monica:
RAND Corporation, 2011).

17. C. Gilson, K. Roberts, E. Weymes, and M. Pratt, *Peak Performance:
Business Lessons from the World's Top Sports Organizations* (London: Harper
Collins Business, 2001).

18. Ibid., 388.

Chapter 5

1. M. Lewis, *Moneyball: The Art of Winning an Unfair Game* (New York: Norton, 2004).
2. B. Gates, "My Plan to Fix the World's Biggest Problems," *The Wall Street Journal*, January 25, 2013, online.wsj.com/news/articles/SB100014241278 87323539804578261780648285770.
3. C. DeRose and N. M. Tichy, *Judgment on the Front Line: How Smart Companies Win by Trusting Their People* (New York: Portfolio/Penguin, 2012).
4. F. Foer, *How Soccer Explains the World* (New York: HarperCollins, 2004). The ensuing quotations come from pp. 159–160, respectively.
5. See J. Wilson, *Inverting the Pyramid: the History of Soccer Tactics* (New York: Nation Books, 2013) for specific targets that Lobanovsky set depending on whether the team was "pressing" or "squeezing."
6. M. Aslett, "Valeryi Lobanovskyi: Soccer Manager . . . Big Data Visionary," December, 2011, blogs.the451group.com/information_management/2011/12/16/valeriy-lobanovskyi/. The spelling of Valeri Lobanovsky (Valeryi Lobanovskyi) varies with different sources.
7. A report by COSO (Committee of Sponsoring Organizations of the Treadway Commission) covering the period 1998–2007 was retrieved from www.coso.org/FraudReport.htm.
8. BBC News, "Targets 'Destroy Trust in Police.'" BBC News—Home, December 15, 2007, news.bbc.co.uk/1/hi/uk/7145860.stm.
9. J. Seddon, *Systems Thinking in the Public Sector: The Failure of the Reform Regime . . . and a Manifesto for a Better Way* (Axminster, UK: Triarchy Press, 2008).
10. C. Wolmar, *Broken Rails: How Privatisation Wrecked Britain's Railways* (London: Aurum, 2001).
11. CNN, "Former Atlanta Schools Superintendent Reports to Jail in Cheating Scandal," April 3, 2013, edition.cnn.com/2013/04/02/justice/georgia-cheating-scandal/.
12. Full details of the Adequate Yearly Progress requirements were retrieved from www.ncpie.org/nclbaction/ayp.html.
13. In 1993 the UK government established the Office for Standards in Education (OFSTED). It is an independent government agency that inspects all schools in England. Reports judge schools in four categories. If a school is judged as "Inadequate," the lowest category, then it will be closely monitored by Ofsted until it improves. This involves further inspections every ten weeks. If the school fails to improve rapidly then the head is usually fired and/or the school may be closed or reconstituted.

14. D. T. Campbell, *Assessing the Impact of Planned Social Change* (Kalamazoo: Evaluation Center, College of Education, Western Michigan University, 1976).

15. One Everest expedition in 1996 and its fate is vividly documented in J. Krakauer, *Into Thin Air: A Personal Account of the Mt. Everest Disaster* (New York: Anchor Books, 1999). Krakauer's personal views caused controversy among other climbers who were on the mountain at the same time and were not injured. Calculated risk has always been part of the appeal of climbing, for those who climb mountains, so the idea of "summit fever" is not endorsed unanimously in that community.

16. L. D. Ordóñez, M. E. Schweitzer, A. D. Galinsky, and M. H. Bazerman, "Goals Gone Wild: The Systematic Side Effects of Overprescribing Goal Setting," *The Academy of Management Perspectives* 23, No. 1 (2009):6–16.

17. Y. Sheffi, *The Resilient Enterprise: Overcoming Vulnerability for Competitive Advantage* (Cambridge, MA: MIT Press, 2005).

18. On the importance of balanced scorecards, see R. S. Kaplan and D. P. Norton, Using the balanced scorecard as a strategic management system. *Harvard Business Review* 74, No. 1 (1996): 75–85. Also see J. Elkington, *Cannibals with Forks: The Triple Bottom Line of 21st Century Business* (London: Capstone, 1997).

19. All data, quotations, and information about Shoebuy.com on this page and the following pages were collected from primary sources during the Performance Beyond Expectations research, unless otherwise indicated; see Appendix.

20. See www.oecd.org/pisa/.

21. This argument and the ensuing analysis is present in several of the increasing number of accounts of Finnish educational success. The most well-documented analysis is by Finnish educational expert Pasi Sahlberg, currently professor at the Harvard Graduate School of Education and winner of the $100,000 2012 Grawemeyer Award for the best book or idea in education. See P. Sahlberg, *Finnish Lessons: What Can the World Learn from Educational Change in Finland?* (New York: Teachers College Press, 2012).

22. From personal communication between P. Sahlberg and A. Hargreaves.

23. The best book and most current evidence on this issue is in A. Datnow and V. Park, *Data-Driven Leadership* (San Francisco: Wiley, 2014).

24. The full report of the research in Ontario on which the following text draws is in A. Hargreaves and H. Braun, "Leading for All: A Research Report of the Development, Design, Implementation and Impact of Ontario's 'Essential for Some, Good for All' Initiative" (Oakville: Council

of Ontario Directors of Education, 2012). Ontario's performance on the PISA tests compared to other Canadian provinces at the time of the research is reported in T. Knighton, P. Brochu, and T. Gluszynski, *Measuring Up: Canadian Results of the OECD PISA Study* (Ottawa, Ontario: Statistics Canada, 2010).

25. These gains on the province's own internal measures have been identified by many authors and organizations. The most authoritative source is from international expert in leadership and change, and former Special Advisor to the premier of Ontario on education, Michael Fullan. See M. Fullan and A. Boyle, *Big-City School Reforms: Lessons From New York, Toronto and London* (New York: Teachers' College Press, 2014).

26. V. Mayer-Schonberger and K. Cukier, *Big Data: A Revolution That Will Transform How We Live, Work and Think* (New York: Houghton Mifflin, 2013).

27. Mayer-Schonberger and Cukier, 196.

28. R. L. Arar Han, *Tanpin Kanri: Retail Practice at Seven Eleven Japan*, Harvard Business School case study (Cambridge, MA: Harvard Business School, 2005).

Chapter 6

1. The issues of sustainability and sustainable leadership are discussed at length in A. Hargreaves, and D. Fink, *Sustainable Leadership* (San Francisco: Jossey-Bass, 2006).

2. J. Collins, *How the Mighty Fall* (New York: HarperCollins, 2009).

3. All data, direct quotations, and information about Marks & Spencer on this page and following pages were collected from primary sources during the Performance Beyond Expectations research, supplemented by information from corporate websites, news stories, and from J. Bevan, *The Rise and Fall of Marks & Spencer: And How It Rose Again* (London: Profile Books, 2007).

4. "M&S Tops Reputation Institute's Rankings for Best Corporate Reputation," *Reputation Institute*, June 4, 2009, www.reputationinstitute. com/events/RI_Press%20Release_GLOBAL_PULSE_UK_04june 2009.pdf.

Other performance data at the time of our study were retrieved from Markets data: Marks & Spencer Group PLC, *Financial Times*, August 13, 2010, http://markets.ft.com/tearsheets/performance.asp?s=uk:MKS;

Marks & Spencer. (2009). *Annual Report 2010: Key Performance Measures*, annualreport.marksandspencer.com/financial-statements/key-performance-measures.aspx

"Recession Over: GDP Growth Revised Higher as M&S Claims the Worst of the Downturn Is Behind Us," *Mail Online*, May 25, 2010, www.dailymail.co.uk/news/article-1281221/Marks-Spencer-proclaims-worst-recession-rings-632m-profit.html; Williams, H. (2010, May 25). "Marks & Spencer report £632m profit," *The Independent*, May 25, 2010, www.independent.co.uk/news/business/news/marks-amp-spencer-report-pound632m-profit-1982252.html.

5. For instance, in its 2005 report on Corporate Social Responsibility, M&S reported that it had been "the leading retailer in the global Dow Jones Sustainability Index in 2003, 2004 and 2005." See Marks & Spencer, *Corporate Social Responsibility Report*, 2005, 2, http://corporate.marksandspencer.com/documents/publications/2005/2005_csr_report.pdf.

6. Bevan, 202.

7. Ibid., 177–178.

8. Ibid., 213.

9. R. G. Eccles, G. Serafeim, & K. Armbrester, *Tough Decisions at Marks & Spencer*, Harvard Business School case study (Cambridge, MA: Harvard Business School, 2012), 2.

10. The full report on this visit and study is presented in A. Hargreaves, G. Halász, and B. Pont, "The Finnish Approach to System Leadership," in *Improving School Leadership, Vol. 2: Case Studies on System Leadership*, ed. B. Pont, D. Nusche, and D. Hopkins (Paris: OECD, 2008), 69–109.

11. Several reports commenting on Finnish success have been published by international policy and policy advisory bodies; see OECD, "Finland: Slow and Steady Reform for Consistently High Results," in *Strong Performers and Successful Reformers in Education: Lessons from PISA for the United States* (Paris: OECD, 2011),117–136; M. Mourshed, C. Chijioke, and M. Barber, *How the World's Most Improved School Systems Keep Getting Better* (London: McKinsey, 2010).

12. Other aspects of the visit to Jarvenpaa are recorded in Hargreaves, Halasz, and Pont, "The Finnish Approach to System Leadership."

13. See P. Sahlberg, *Finnish Lessons: What Can the World Learn from Educational Change in Finland?* (New York: Teachers College Press, 2011).

14. Ibid., 6.

15. On special education issues in Finland, see N. Grubb, H. Marit Jahr, J. Neumuller, and S. Field, *Equity in Education: Thematic Review of Finland* (Paris: OECD, 2005).

16. OECD, *PISA 2012 Results in Focus: What 15-Year-Olds Know and What They Can Do with What They Know* (Paris: OECD, 2013), accessed from www.oecd.org/pisa/keyfindings/pisa-2012-results-overview.pdf.

17. See for example, A. Taylor, "Finland Used to Have the Best Educational System in the World: What Happened?" *Business Insider*, December 3, 2013, www.businessinsider.com/why-finland-fell-in-the-pisa-rankings-2013–12.

18. D. Woods, C. Husbands, and C. Brown, *Transforming Education for All: The Tower Hamlets Story* (London: Tower Hamlets, 2013)

19. S. Mesure, "Stuart Rose: Fine and Dandy," *The Independent* (February 10, 2007), www.independent.co.uk/news/people/profiles/stuart-rose-fine-and-dandy-435791.html.

20. See Sir S. Rose on the changing role of business leaders, in *The Guardian* (March 29, 2012), www.theguardian.com/sustainable-business/sir-stuart-rose-changing-role-business-leaders.

21. Quotation from an interview with Sir Stuart Rose published by The Marketing Society (January 2013), www.marketingsociety.co.uk/the-library/interview-sir-stuart-rose.

22. S. Rose, "Staying Green in a Tough Economic Climate," *HBR Green, Harvard Business Review* (March 4, 2008), www.hbrgreen.org/2008/03/the_hard_economics_of_green.html.

23. E. Abrahamson, *Change Without Pain: How Managers Can Overcome Initiative Overload, Organizational Chaos, and Employee Burnout* (Boston: Harvard Business Press, 2004), 23.

24. Abrahamson, 10.

25. D. Dodd and K. Favaro, *The Three Tensions: Winning the Struggle to Perform Without Compromise* (San Francisco: Wiley, 2007), 75.

26. Ibid., 77.

27. J. Kotter, *Leading Change* (Cambridge, MA: Harvard Business School Press, 1996), 122–124.

28. J. M. Keynes, *A Tract on Monetary Reform* (London: Macmillan, 1923), 80.

29. World Commission on Environment and Development, *Our Common Future* (New York: United Nations General Assembly, 1987).

Chapter 7

1. M. Kets de Vries, *The Leader on the Couch: A Clinical Approach to Changing People and Organizations* (San Francisco: Wiley, 2006), 17.
2. Dylan's song, "Desolation Row," was recorded in 1965 on his album *Highway 61 Revisited.*
3. Max Weber described three forms of authority—charismatic, traditional, and legal—as rational or bureaucratic or legal-rational, in M. Weber, "The Three Types of Legitimate Authority," *Berkeley Publications in Society and Institutions* 4, No. 1 (1958): 1–11. Translated by Hans Gerth.
4. These and all other references in this paragraph come from M. Kets De Vries, January 7, 2014, blogs.hbr.org/2014/01/is-your-boss-a-psychopath/
5. Kets de Vries, 141.
6. See O. Burkeman, *The Antidote: Happiness for People Who Can't Stand Positive Thinking* (New York: Faber and Faber, 2012).
7. Retrieved from www.dailygood.org/story/466/gandhi-s-10-rules-for-changing-the-world-henrik-edberg/.
8. This quote is widely attributed to Wayne Gretsky, particularly among hockey fans. Its source is from an interview with Bob MacKenzie, editor, in *Hockey News*, January 16, 1983.
9. Retrieved from www.kipling.org.uk/poems_if.htm.
10. R. M. Pirsig, *Zen and the Art of Motorcycle Maintenance: An Inquiry into Values* (New York: William Morrow, 1974).
11. Arreguin-Toft, 104.
12. See A. Boynton and B. Fisher, B., *Virtuoso Teams: Lessons from Teams That Changed Their Worlds* (New York: Prentice Hall, 2005).
13. Cited in I. Calvino, *Invisible Cities* (Boston: Houghton Mifflin, 1978).
14. M. Montessori, *The Absorbent Mind* (Whitebridge, MT: Kessinger, 2004). Originally published 1949.

Appendix

1. *Performance Beyond Expectations*, codirected by Andy Hargreaves (Boston College, USA) and Alma Harris (at the London Institute of Education) (Nottingham, England: NCSL, 2011). Research team: Alan Boyle, Michelle De La Rosa, Kathryn Ghent, Janet Goodall, Alex Gurn, and Lori McEwen. The project was funded by the National College for School Leadership and the Specialist Schools and Academies Trust in England.

   Review of "Essential for Some, Good for All" in Ontario, codirected by Andy Hargreaves and Henry Braun. Research team: Lauren Chapman,

Maureen Hughes, Karen Lam, Beth Morgan, Kathryn Sallis, Adam Steiner, Matt Welch, and Yu Jin Lee. Funded by the Council of Directors in Education, in Ontario, Canada.

OECD Review of School Leadership and School Improvement in Finland. Research Team with Andy Hargreaves; Beatrice Pont of the Organization for Economic Cooperation and Development (OECD); and Gabor Halasz, formerly Deputy Minister of Education in Hungary.

A Revolution in a Decade: Ten out of Ten. Research Project led by Alan Boyle and Salli Humphreys (London: Leannta, 2012).

Review of Singapore Educational System, codirected by Andy Hargreaves and Pak Tee Ng (National Institute of Education, Singapore). Funding support from the National Institute of Education, Singapore.

2. A. Hargreaves and A. Harris, *Performance Beyond Expectations* (Nottingham, England: NCSL, 2011).

3. Ibid.

4. Ibid., 45.

5. Andy Hargreaves was visiting professor at The National Institute of Education in Singapore during 2011.

6. A. Hargreaves, G. Halász, and B. Pont, "The Finnish Approach to System Leadership," in *Improving School Leadership, Vol. 2: Case Studies on System Leadership,* ed. B. Pont, D. Nusche, and D. Hopkins (Paris: OECD, 2008), 69–109.

7. A. Hargreaves and H. Braun, *Leading for All: A Research Report of the Development, Design, Implementation and Impact of Ontario's "Essential for Some, Good for All" Initiative* (Ontario: Council of Ontario Directors of Education, 2012).

8. See A. Boyle and S. Humphreys, *A Revolution in a Decade: Ten out of Ten* (London: Leannta, 2012).

Acknowledgments

The idea of uplifting leadership did not come out of thin air or off the top of our heads. The material in this book came from extensive research encompassing large data sets from many different organizations with invaluable contributions from many people over a number of years.

We are particularly grateful to Steve Munby and Sue Williamson—people who are committed to our own dream of identifying and spreading the lessons of uplifting leadership; and also to the organizations they have led (National College for School Leadership and Specialist Schools and Academies Trust) who funded much of the research work.

Very special thanks go to the over three hundred uplifting leaders we met in the companies, sports organizations, and education systems we visited, who inspired us with their words and actions, openly engaged with us in conversation, and devoted precious time and energy to our visits.

We were fortunate to work with some amazing coinvestigators and research teams on both sides of the globe on the projects where the ideas in this book originated. The *Performing Beyond Expectations* study from which this book first originated was codirected by Andy Hargreaves at Boston College and Alma Harris at the London Institute of Education through Grant # 5001068 at Boston College. The research team comprised Alan Boyle,

Michelle De La Rosa, Kathryn Ghent, Janet Goodall, Alex Gurn, Corrie Stone Johnson, and Lori McEwen. Research added to this original project involved Dennis Shirley as coresearcher of the California Teachers' Association, Pak Tee Ng as coresearcher of the Singapore educational system; and Alex Gurn of the Vancouver Giants.

Data on the Ontario educational system were first collected and analyzed in a *Review of Essential for Some Good for All*, the province's special education strategy. The review was codirected by Andy Hargreaves and Henry Braun. The research team comprised Lauren Chapman, Maureen Hughes, Karen Lam, Beth Morgan, Kathryn Sallis, Adam Steiner, Matt Welch, and Yu Jin Lee. The project was funded by the Council of Directors in Education, in Ontario, Canada.

A Revolution in a Decade: Ten Out of Ten—a long-term review of the work of The Learning Trust in Hackney—was conducted by Alan Boyle and Salli Humphreys and funded by Leannta Education Associates.

In the closing stages of completing this manuscript, Brad Kershner, Meredith Moore, Adam Steiner, and Luke Reynolds helped us with a lot of essential final fact checking. Kristie Thayer managed to move masses of information across to California in the face of many obstacles, including heavy snow. Elizabeth Cox carried out viral background research on the social and cultural origins of uplift in U.S. history. The editorial team at Jossey-Bass—Senior Editor Karen Murphy, Assistant Editor John Maas, Development Editor Christine Moore, Senior Production Editor Mark Karmendy, and Copyeditor Donna J. Weinson— expertly enabled us to tighten and focus our manuscript to get our message across in the best possible way, and they were relentless in ensuring that all the necessary work was accomplished so that the book could make its production deadlines.

The Authors

Andy Hargreaves is the Thomas More Brennan Chair in Education at the Lynch School of Education at Boston College. Before that, he was the cofounder and codirector of the International Centre for Educational Change at the Ontario Institute for Studies in Education. In 2014, he was ranked as one of the twelve most influential scholars on US public education policy.

Andy has written or edited more than twenty-five books on leadership and change. They include *Sustainable Leadership* (with Dean Fink; Wiley, 2006) and *Professional Capital* (with Michael Fullan; Teachers' College Press, 2012). His books have received outstanding book awards at the International Leadership Association, and from the American Libraries Association, the National Staff Development Council, the American Educational Research Association, and the American Association of Colleges for Teacher Education. They are translated into many languages.

Andy has held visiting professorships in the United States, United Kingdom, Canada, Singapore, Hong Kong, Sweden, and Japan. His awards include an Honorary Doctorate from Scandinavia's oldest university (Uppsala). Andy has consulted widely with large-scale organizations and systems across the world such as the World Bank and the Organization for Economic Cooperation and Development (OECD) and is in high demand as a keynote speaker where he has delivered addresses in forty-four

US States, forty-three countries, and all Canadian and Australian states and provinces.

You can follow Andy on twitter @HargreavesBC. For more information, and to see his TEDx talk on Uplifting Leadership, please visit www.andyhargreaves.com.

•   •   •

Alan Boyle is director of Leannta Education Associates, a company he founded fourteen years ago. As a leadership consultant he designs and creates professional learning for education leaders in the United Kingdom and abroad. Over the last twelve years he has established and maintained learning partnerships between school district leaders in the United Kingdom and North America. Between 2006 and 2008 he worked as a consultant to the Department of Education in New York City to establish the Quality Review process in all schools across the city. As a researcher, his latest work involved an in-depth analysis of systemwide reforms across New York City, Toronto, and London over the decade 2002–2012. Alan is a qualified consultant and trainer for the EFQM Excellence Model, the European equivalent of the Baldridge Award.

Alan started his career as a science teacher and spent twenty years in urban schools across England. He worked for the National Curriculum Council in England before moving into school district administration, including seven years as the chief inspector of a London borough. He has written science text books and many articles in journals and newspapers. His latest coauthored books are *Big-City School Reforms: Lessons from New York, Toronto and London* (with Michael Fullan; Teachers' College Press, 2014) and *A Revolution in a Decade: Ten Out of Ten* (with Salli Humphreys; Leannta Publishing, 2012). Alan is an invited presenter at international leadership conferences. He was awarded a Winston

Churchill Fellowship in 1982. For more information, please visit www.leannta.com.

• • •

Dr. Alma Harris is professor and director of the Institute of Educational Leadership at the University of Malaysia. She is also Pro-Director (Leadership) at the Institute of Education, University of London. In 2010/12 she was a senior policy adviser to the Welsh government and assisted with the process of national system reform. Her research work focuses primarily on leading organizational change and transformation. Alma is internationally known for her work on school improvement, focusing particularly on improving schools in challenging circumstances. She has also written extensively about leadership in schools and is an expert on the theme of distributed leadership. Her book *Distributed Leadership in Schools: Developing the Leaders of Tomorrow* (published in 2008 by Routledge & Falmer Press) has been translated into several languages. She is president of the International Congress of School Effectiveness and School Improvement and currently holds visiting professorships at the Moscow Higher School of Economics and Nottingham Business School. Her latest book is *Distributed Leadership Matters* (2013) published by Corwin Press.

For more information, please follow Alma on Twitter at @almaharris1 and please visit www.almaharris.co.uk.

Index

A

A/B testing, at Shoebuy.com, 127

Academic Performance Index (API),
    measuring progress in California
    schools, 27

academies (UK)
    competition and collaboration in
        education, 78–79
    The Learning Trust creating, 80–81

accountability, cultural values at
    Scott Bader, 101

actions, uplifting. *see* journey to
    higher performance

African American example, of social
    and community uplift, 4

Agnelli, Gianni, 20, 149

Agnelli, Giovanni, 20

Ahrendts, Angela, 61–64

*The Antidote: Happiness for People
    Who Can't Stand Positive
    Thinking* (Burkeman), 162–163

anxiety. *see* fears

API (Academic Performance Index),
    measuring progress in California
    schools, 27

Apple
    going against the grain, 47

innovation at, 65

assets, understanding and
    appreciating, 174

Australian cricket. *see* Cricket
    Australia

auto-industry
    dark side of data and, 122–123
    Fiat example of dreaming and
        believing, 19–23

B

Bader, Ernest, 96–98

Bailey, Christopher, 63

balanced scorecards
    adopting, 173
    intelligence in approach to
        performance data, 124

Beane, Billy, 115

believing. *see* dreaming and believing

benchmarking, in understanding
    competitors, 169

Benz, Nick, 50, 52–54

Big Data (Mayer-Schonberger and
    Cukier), 133–134

Boyle, Alan, 210–211

Britton, Ian, 38–39

Bruce, Philip, 99–101

bullwhip effect
avoiding, 173
dark side of data and, 123
Burberry
capitalizing on historical core
business, 62–63
history and tradition of, 61
makeover in approach to luxury
market, 63–64
Burkeman, Oliver, 162–163
Burnley Football Club
building on club tradition, 38
connecting to community of
supporters, 40–41
crisis leading to will to change,
38–39
performance metrics, 118–119
players and coaches role in
turnaround, 41–42
"prodigal leadership" process at,
150
redefining club purpose, 37
burnout, sustainable growth in
avoiding, 174
business practices, balancing with
creativity (Dogfish Head Craft
Brewery), 52–54

C
Calagione, Mariah, 51–53, 153, 164
Calagione, Sam
example of strong leadership, 164
improbable match with Nick Benz,
52–54
innovation in use of ingredients in
beer, 50–51
orientation to feasible growth
rates, 154
role in starting Dogfish Head Craft
Brewery, 48–49
valuing co-opetition, 77–78
Campbell, Donald T., 122
Campbell's Law, 122, 131
capital, Ernest Bader's belief in labor's
ownership of, 96–97
challenges, courage in response to,
25–26. see also hard work
Change Without Pain
(Abrahamson), 152
charismatic leaders
achieving success based on
foundations previously
established, 149
not same as uplifting leadership,
163
positive and negative examples,
161–162
Weber on, 161
charity
Ernest Bader's vision and, 98
Scott Bader donations to, 100
charter schools, 78–79
Chrysler, partnership with Fiat,
20–23
Churchill, Winston, 33
Clif Bar, 24
cliques, avoiding, 171
Cochrane, Josephine, 32–33
Cody, Brian, 105–106
collaboration with competition
benchmarking in understanding
competitors, 169
conclusion, 90–91
co-opetition examples, 77–78
co-opetition overview, 71–72
Cricket Australia example, 72–75

DuPont example, 35
Ernest Bader's belief in
    collaboration rather than
    conflict, 97
European Airbus Consortium
    example, 76
factors in uplifting organizations,
    9–10
Fiat example, 76–77
giving your best ideas away,
    168–169
helping and respecting the
    competition, 169
The Learning Trust and, 79–81
McClelland's needs as drivers of
    performance, 69
Nashville schools example,
    84–86
overview of, 12
relationship between competition
    and cooperation, 67–68
school-to-school federations,
    81–84
seeking higher common ground
    with competitors, 169
Silicon Valley example, 76
Singapore example, 86–90
Tower Hamlets example, 110–111
ways in which competition and
    collaboration can work together,
    70–71
collective identity, from common
    dream, 19
collective ownership, of
    commonwealth, 96
collective responsibility, cultural
    values at Scott Bader, 101
Collins, Jim, 51

Collins, Kevan, 109–110, 149
common ground, seeking higher
    common ground with
    competition, 169
commonwealth. see also Scott Bader
    collective ownership, 96
    power of pull in, 98
community uplift. see social and
    community uplift
competition
    benchmarking in understanding
        competitors, 169
    collaboration with. see
        collaboration with competition
    helping and respecting, 169
    killing the competition as
        obstacle to sustainable success,
        143–144
    monopolies and, 89
    seeking higher common ground
        with, 169
    in Singapore education system,
        86–87
complacency
    Finnish example, 147–148
    obstacles to sustainable success,
        142–143
co-opetition
    Cricket Australia example, 72–75
    European Airbus Consortium
        example, 76
    Fiat example, 76–77
    overview of, 71–72
    Silicon Valley example, 76
    transcendent value created by,
        77–78
Co-opetition (Brandenburger and
    Nalebuff), 76

counter-flow. *see* creativity and
counter-flow
courage, 25–26. *see also* dreaming
and daring
Coyle, Owen, 41–42
creative pathways, forging, 11
creativity and counter-flow
Burberry example, 61–64
Dogfish Head Craft Brewery
example, 48–54
DuPont tradition of innovation,
34–35
Dyson example, 55
factors in uplifting organizations,
9–10
Finnish composers as example
of, 145
going against the grain, 47–55
industries going against the grain,
47–48
Lobansky's system stifling
creativity, 118
overview of, 11–12
Singapore example, 56–58
surprise tactics, 167
surprising yourself, 167–168
taking the opposite approach, 45–47
Teach Less, Learn More initiative
in Singapore, 58–61
teaching less and learning more,
55–56
trial and error approach, 168
Cricket Australia
co-opetition example, 72–75
hubris and complacency as
obstacles to sustainable
success, 142
necessity of competition in
sustaining success, 143

"prodigal leadership" process,
150
understanding link between
short and long-term
improvement, 156
crisis, leading to will to change
Burnley example, 38–39
DuPont example, 34
Finnish example, 145–146
Scott Bader example, 99–101
Crossley, David, 85–86
CTA (California Teachers'
Association)
competition and collaboration
and, 78–79
converting teachers into leaders,
29–31
dealing with negative perception
of teachers, 27–28
expanding the audience of the PBE
study, 179
role in turning around California
schools, 26–27
struggling with the opposition of
Governor Schwarzenegger, 28
cultural changes, at Scott Bader,
101–102

D
daring. *see* dreaming and daring
data. *see also* measurements,
meaningful
abuses of, 116–117
interpreting intelligently, 173
minding data with intelligence,
124
permeating presence in current
world, 113–114
Data Point Capital, 126

Davies, Siân, 81–82
deadlines, qualities of uplifting organizations and, 9
determination. *see* dreaming with determination
dignity, in conducting difficult conversations, 172
"disciplined innovation" (Collins), 51
discrimination, inspiring dreams and, 19
Dodd, Dominic, 155
Dogfish Head Craft Brewery
  balancing creativity with good business, 52–54
  creative use of unusual ingredients, 50–51
  eccentric style at, 51
  example of creativity, 12
  example of sustainable success, 14
  feasible growth rates at, 153
  passion for innovation, 49
  promoting success of competitors, 77–78
  taking on industry giants by going a different direction, 48
  understanding link between short and long-term improvement, 156
"Dogfish Way," 95–96
doing. *see* dreaming and doing
dreaming and believing
  Clif Bar example, 24
  conclusion, 24–25
  FIAT example, 19–23
  inspiration and, 18–19
  Martin Luther King example, 17–18

US women's soccer team example, 23
dreaming and daring
  articulating a common vision, 164–165
  CTA (California Teachers' Association) example, 26–32
  Josephine Cochrane example, 32–33
  overview of, 25
  response to challenges and opposition, 25–26
dreaming and doing
  Burnley Football Club example, 37–42
  DuPont example, 34–37
  overview of, 33
  value of endurance, 33–34
dreaming with determination
  articulating a common vision, 164–165
  being neither fearful or fearless, 165–166
  bringing your dream to life, 165
  conclusion, 42–43
  dreaming and believing. *see* dreaming and believing
  dreaming and daring. *see* dreaming and daring
  dreaming and doing. *see* dreaming and doing
  factors in uplifting organizations, 9–10
  fighting for what is right, 166
  overview of, 10–11
  understanding fears of others, 166–167
drop shipment model, Shoebuy.com, 125–126

DuPont
 benefits of thinking differently,
  35–36
 consistency in open, positive
  communication, 36
 example of collaboration with
  competition, 88–89
 financial crisis and, 34
 historical resiliency of, 36–37
 tradition of innovation, 34–35
Dyche, Sean, 42
Dyson, Sir James, 55
Dyson example, of creativity and
 counter-flow, 55

E

eccentricity, at Dogfish Head Craft
 Brewery, 51
ecological responsibility. *see*
 environmental responsibility
Edmundson, Dave, 37, 40–41
education. *see* public education
elation, not sufficient by itself,
 162–164
element, being in your
 (Robinson), 47
elites, avoiding, 171
emotional (inspirational)
 leadership, not sufficient by
 itself, 161–164
emotional and spiritual uplift
 Ernest Bader's vision and, 97
 Fiat example, 23
 overview of, 2–4
employees
 empowering, 134
 as partners in commonwealth, 97
endurance, dreaming and doing and,
 33–34

English Premier League, 37–38. *see
 also* Burnley Football Club
Enron, abuses of data, 119
environmental responsibility.
 see also sustainability,
  environmental
 DuPont example, 35
 Fiat example, 22–23
envy, community aspiration vs. envy
 as guiding emotion, 25
equity, inspiring dreams
 and, 18–19
Erikson, Gary, 24
European Airbus Consortium
 example, of co-opetition, 76

F

Fabbrica Italiana Automobili Torino.
 see Fiat (Fabbrica Italiana
  Automobili Torino)
Facebook, Shoebuy.com
 use of, 127
failure, turning into success, 1–2
false starts and recoveries
 Marks & Spencer (M&S) example,
  140–142
 overview of, 138
 Vancouver Giants hockey team as
  example, 138–140
Favaro, Ken, 155
fears
 being neither fearful or fearless,
  165–166
 understanding fears of others,
  166–167
federations
 Nashville schools example,
  84–86
 in UK, 81–84

Fiat (FabbricaItalianaAutomobili
  Torino)
  creating foundations for success
    at, 149
  example of co-opetition, 76–77
  example of dreaming and
    believing, 19–23
  example of going against the
    grain, 47
  hubris and complacency as
    obstacles to sustainable success,
    142–143
  necessity of competition in
    sustaining success, 143
  team building at, 95
The Fifth Discipline (Senge), 36
Finnish Lessons (Sahlberg), 146
Finland, public education in
  emphasis of teaching rather than
    testing, 129–130
  linking parallel research to PBE
    study, 179
  political stability linked to success
    in, 149
  signs of complacency, 147–148
  sustainable success, 144–147
Fletcher, Paul, 41
Fogarty, Martin, 106
Ford, Henry, 19–20, 56
Ford Motor Company, 19–20
free schools (Sweden), 78–79

G
gaming the system, abuses of
  performance metrics, 119–120
Gates, Bill, 32, 115–116
Gersch, Kathy, 64
Gilbert, Christine, 108–110, 149
Global Collaboratory (DuPont), 35, 88

globalization, localization and, 88
goals
  Goals Gone Wild, 122–123
  qualities of uplifting organizations
    and, 8
  relationship to heritage or
    history, 19
Goals Gone Wild, 122–123
Goh Chok Tong, 58
Greensbury, Sir Richard, 141
growth rates
  feasible, 153–154
  growing at sustainable rates,
    174–175

H
Hackney schools
  The Learning Trust role in
    turnaround, 79–81
  linking to parallel research to PBE
    study, 180
  maintaining continuity with past
    during turnarounds, 153
  school-to-school federations,
    81–84
  understanding link between short
    and long-term improvement,
    155–156
hard processes, approaches to
  turnaround and uplift, 15
hard work
  combining with soft process in
    performance improvement, 5
  CTA struggle with the opposition
    of Governor Schwarzenegger, 28
  Finnish value of sisu (persistence
    despite obstacles), 147
  struggle as part of leadership, 166
Hargreaves, Andy, 179, 209–210

Harris, Dr. Alma, 211
He Said Beer, She Said Wine
  (Calagione), 77
Heins, Eric, 26–31
heritage
  Burberry basing turnaround on
    tradition, 61–63
  Burnley Football Club building on
    tradition, 38
  connecting to, 173–174
  M&S example, 151
  maintaining continuity with past
    during turnarounds, 152–153
  "prodigal leadership" process and,
    150–152
  role in inspiring dreams, 19
high pressure, qualities of uplifting
  organizations and, 8–9
honesty, being transparent in use of
  metrics, 172–173
How Soccer Changed the World (Foer),
  117
How the Weak Win Wars (Arreguin-
  Toft), 45–46, 167
hubris, obstacles to sustainable
  success, 142–143
hurling
  Kilkenny example of building team
    spirit, 105–106
  overview and history of, 103–105

I
IDEO, 55
indicators, measuring with meaning,
  13. *see also* performance metrics
innovation
  at Apple, 65
  at Dogfish Head Craft Brewery,
    49–51

at DuPont, 34–35
education in Finland promoting,
  146–147
paradoxical relationship to
  improvement, 56
trial and error approach and, 168
inspiration
  dreaming and believing and,
    18–19
  not sufficient by itself, 161–164
inspirational leadership, 163. *see also*
  charismatic leaders
intellectual property rights, securing
  and sharing, 168–169
inventory, Shoebuy.com approach to,
  125–127
iPhone, example of going against the
  grain, 47

J
Jobs, Steve, 32
journey to higher performance
  avoiding cliques and elites, 171
  being neither fearful or fearless,
    165–166
  being transparent in use of metrics,
    172–173
  benchmarking in understanding
    competitors, 169
  bringing dreams to life, 165
  building trust, 170–171
  conducting difficult conversations
    with dignity, 172
  connecting short-term results to
    long-term dreams, 175
  connecting to heritage or
    traditions, 173–174
  converting weaknesses into
    strengths, 171

daring to dream, 164–165

emotion or elation not sufficient by itself, 161–164

fighting for what is right, 166

getting the best from teams, 170

giving your best ideas away, 168–169

growing at sustainable rates, 174–175

helping and respecting the competition, 169

interpreting data intelligently, 173

knowing/being concerned with your people's welfare, 170

making metrics meaningful, 173

measuring what you value, 172

overview of, 14–16

quest for uplift, 159–161

seeking higher common ground with competitors, 169

sharing/communicating targets, 172

staying aloft (uplifted), 175–176

staying grounded, 164, 171

surprising yourself, 167–168

trial and error approach to innovation, 168

understanding and appreciating assets, 174

understanding fears of others, 166–167

using surprise tactics, 167

Judgment on the Front Line: How Smart Companies Win by Trusting Their People (DeRose and Tichy), 116

K

Kanter, Rosabeth Moss, 77

Keller, Jim, 126

Kelley, David, 55

Kelley, Tom, 55

key performance indicators (KPIs)

qualities of uplifting organizations and, 8

sharing your targets, 172

Keynes, John Maynard, 156

Kilby, Barry, 37, 39–40, 150

Kilfrost example, of collaboration with competition, 88–89

King Jr., Martin Luther, 4, 17–18

Kotter, John, 155

KPIs (key performance indicators)

qualities of uplifting organizations and, 8

sharing your targets, 172

Kullman, Ellen, 34–36, 88–89

L

The Leader on the Couch (de Vries), 161–162

Leadership and the Art of Struggle (Snyder), 32

learning

Singapore initiative and, 58–61

teaching less and learning more, 55–56

The Learning Trust

addressing Hackney schools, 79–81

example of collaboration with competition, 12

linking to parallel research to PBE study, 180

role in creating school-to-school federations in UK, 81–84

Lee Kwan Yew, 56

legacy of leadership, 150–152

life changing quality, of inspiring dreams, 18

Lift (Ryan and Quinn), 2
Lim, Adrian, 59–60, 87, 149, 153
Lincoln, Abraham, 32
Lobansky, Valeri, 117–118
localization, globalization and, 88
long-term improvements
    connecting short-term results to,
        175
    sustainable success and, 155–156
luxury apparel market
    Burberry's counter-flow strategy,
        63–64
    Burberry's loss of focus, 61

M
M&S. *see* Marks & Spencer (M&S)
Mandela, Nelson, 3
Marchionne, Sergio, 21–23, 77, 149
market-driven science, in DuPont
    tradition, 34–35
Markham, Dan, 73–75
Marks, Michael, 140
Marks & Spencer (M&S)
    dreaming with determination
        at, 11
    nonsustainability example,
        140–142
    "prodigal leadership" example
        (Sir Stuart Rose), 150–152
    team building at, 95
measurements, meaningful
    abuses of metrics, 116–117
    bullwhip effect and, 123
    Burnley Football Club example,
        118–119
    Campbell's Law, 122
    conclusion, 132–135
    controversies regarding tests in
        public education, 129–132

dark side of data, 123
factors in uplifting organizations,
    9–10
gaming the system and, 119–120
improving human conditions
    (Gates on), 115–116
interpreting data intelligently,
    124, 173
life and death consequences of
    performance targets, 122–123
Lobansky's system of performance
    metrics, 117–118
making metrics meaningful, 173
measuring what you value, 172
Oakland As example, 114–115
overview of, 13–14
permeating presence of data today,
    113–114
sharing/communicating targets,
    172
Shoebuy.com example, 124–129
testing students and, 121
transparency in use of metrics,
    172–173
merit pay program, in New York City
    public education, 111
metrics. *see* measurements,
    meaningful; performance
    metrics
milestones, 8
Millennium Goals, 116
Moneyball (Lewis), 114–115,
    117, 132
Mother Teresa, examples of
    emotional and spiritual uplift, 3
motivational value
    of being on collaborative edge, 91
    Singapore education and, 86–90
mutual respect. *see* respect

N

Nashville schools example, of collaboration with competition, 84–86

National Institute of Education (Singapore). *see* Singapore, public education in

Ngee Ann Secondary School. *see also* Singapore, public education in
   collaboration with competition example, 87
   creating foundation for success at, 149
   incorporating technology into learning, 59–60

No Child Left Behind Legislation (1996), 120

Nokia, 47, 90, 148

nonsustainability
   false starts and recoveries, 138
   hubris and complacency, 142–143
   killing the competition, 143–144
   Marks & Spencer (M&S) example, 140–142
   overview of, 138
   Vancouver Giants hockey team as example of false starts and recoveries, 138–140

O

Oakland Athletics example, of successful use of data, 114–115

Obama, Barack, 4

obstacles, overcoming. *see* hard work

OECD (Organization for Economic Cooperation and Development) PISA tests. *see* PISA tests, of student achievement

Okoruwa, Tricia, 81–82, 150, 155–156

Ontario, Canada (public education in)
   linking to parallel research to PBE study, 179–180
   political stability linked to success in, 149–150
   testing students and, 130–131

Organization for Economic Cooperation and Development (OECD) PISA tests. *see* PISA tests, of student achievement

Ortega, Mary Rose, 26, 28–31

P

partnerships
   co-opetition and, 76
   workers as partners in common-wealth, 97

PBE (performed beyond expectations) study
   analysis of, 178–179
   case studies in, 177–178
   distilling key elements into six factors, 180
   interviews in, 178
   linking to parallel research, 179–180
   questions asked, 177
   reaching a wide audience, 179
   triangulation of multiple sources of data, 180

performance metrics. *see also* measurements, meaningful
   abuses of, 116
   Burnley Football Club example, 118–119
   Data Point Capital, 126

performance metrics. *see also* measurements, meaningful (*cont'd*)
gaming the system, 119–120
life and death consequences of performance targets, 122–123
Lobansky's use with sports in Soviet Union, 117–118
"performance scouting," Billy Beane's use of data, 115
performance uplift
Fiat example, 23
overview of, 4–6
performed beyond expectations (PBE) study. *see* PBE (performed beyond expectations) study
PISA tests, of student achievement
high scoring nations, 56, 130, 144
political stability linked to success in public education, 149
proper uses of test data, 129
plus-sum games, 76
political stability, success in public education and, 149
The Power of Pull (Hagel, Brown, and Davison), 98
"prodigal leadership"
example of Sir Stuart Rose at M&S, 150–152
sustainable success and, 150
profit sharing, in commonwealth, 97
public education
comparing Eastern and Western approaches, 60–61
competition and collaboration and, 78–79
controversies regarding tests, 129–132

CTA (California Teachers' Association) example, 26–32
emphasis of teaching rather than testing (Finland), 129–130
feasible growth and, 154
Finnish example, 144–148
gaming the system (abuses of performance data), 120
The Learning Trust addressing Hackney schools, 79–81
merit pay program in New York City, 111
Nashville schools example, 84–86
performance improvement examples, 5
political stability linked to success in, 149
school-to-school federations, 81–84
Singapore example, 56–58
Teach Less, Learn More initiative (Singapore), 58–61
teaching less and learning more, 55–56
testing students and, 130–132
Tower Hamlets example, 108–111
public services (police, medical), gaming the system (abuses of performance data), 119
push/pull
avoiding cliques and elites, 171
building trust, 170–171
conclusion, 111–112
conditions in East End (London) and, 106–108
conducting difficult conversations with dignity, 172

converting weaknesses into strengths, 171

factors in uplifting organizations, 9–10

getting the best from teams, 170

Kilkenny example of team building, 105–106

knowing/being concerned with your people's welfare, 170

overview of, 12–13

pulling together, 93–94

pushing each other, 94–95

Scott Bader example. *see* Scott Bader

staying grounded, 171

sticking together, 103–105

team building, 95–96

Tower Hamlets example, 108–111

Q

"quick wins," value of, 155–156

R

relationships

connecting the dots, 175

team building and, 95–96

respect

helping and respecting the competition, 169

teamspirt and, 105–106

results. *see* performance uplift

Robinson, Sir Ken, 47

Rose, Sir Stuart, 95, 150–152

S

Sahlberg, Pasi, 146–147

salaries, differential restrictions in commonwealth, 97

Savitz, Scott, 124, 126–128

scapegoats, avoiding use of, 173

Schwarzenegger, Governor Arnold, 28–32

Scott Bader

balancing causes and community interest with higher purposes, 102–103

being scalable and sustainable, 156

constitution of, 97

cultural changes at, 101–102

Ernest Bader's vision and, 97–98

example of collective identity, 19

financial crisis stimulating changes at, 99–101

history of, 96

hubris and complacency as obstacles to sustainable success, 142

maintaining continuity with past during turnarounds, 153

management structure of, 98

self-doubt, courage in facing, 25–26

Senge, Peter, 36

7-Eleven stores, 134

Sheffi, Yossi, 123

Shoebuy.com

feasible growth rates, 153–154

linking between short and long-term improvements, 156

meaningful use of measurements, 13–14, 124–129

sustainable success, 14

team building, 96

short term improvements

connecting to long-term dreams, 175

sustainable success and, 155–156

Sierra Nevada Ale, 78

Silicon Valley example, of co-opetition, 76

Singapore, public education in
collaborative edge, 86–90
creating foundations for success,
149
economic development based on
changes in, 56–58
expanding the audience of the PBE
study, 179
political stability linked to success
in, 149
successes, 130
Teach Less, Learn More initiative,
58–61
sisu (persistence despite obstacles),
Finnish values, 147
skills
approaches to turnaround and
uplift, 15
soft process in performance
improvement, 5
"small wins," value of, 155–156
Snyder, Steven, 32
social and community uplift
Burnley Football Club example,
40–41
community aspiration vs. envy as
guiding emotion, 25
DuPont example, 35
Fiat example, 23
fighting for what is right, 166
life changing quality of inspiring
dreams, 18–19
overview of, 4
Scott Bader example, 99,
102–103
social decision making, Campbell's
Law and, 122
social media
Burberry use of, 63

Shoebuy.com use of, 127
Sofer, Anne, 149
soft processes (skills)
approaches to turnaround and
uplift, 15
in performance improvement, 5
Sorabella, Mike, 124, 128
Speed, Malcolm, 72–73
Spencer, Thomas, 140
spiritual uplift. see emotional and
spiritual uplift
staff retention, Shoebuy.com, 125
Starble, Craig, 124
Starbucks example, of going against
the grain, 47–48
struggle. see hard work
success, sustaining. see sustainable
success
surprise. see also creativity and
counter-flow
surprising yourself, 167–168
using surprise tactics, 167
sustainability, environmental
Clif Bar example, 24
Fiat example, 22–23
M&S example, 151–152
sustainable success
building foundations of, 148–149
conclusion, 157
connecting short-term results to
long-term dreams, 175
connecting to heritage or
traditions, 173–174
factors in uplifting organizations,
9–10
failure to improve or sustain
success, 138
feasible growth rates, 153–154,
174–175

Finnish education example, 144–148

hubris and complacency as obstacles to, 142–143

killing the competition as obstacle to, 143–144

long and short term improvement, 155–156

maintaining continuity with past during turnarounds, 152–153

Marks & Spencer (M&S) examples, 140–142, 150–152

overview of, 14, 137–138

"prodigal leadership" and, 150

understanding and appreciating assets, 174

Vancouver Giants hockey team example, 138–140

Suzuki, Toshifumi, 134

T

targets (metrics), sharing/ communicating, 172

Teach Less, Learn More initiative, Singapore, 58–61

teachers, as valued profession in Finland, 146

teaching less and learning more overview of, 55–56

Singapore initiative, 58–61

teamwork

getting the best from teams, 170

Ireland Gaelic Athletic Association example, 13

Kilkenny example, 105–106

pulling people together, 103–105

team building, 95–96

technology

Finnish example, 145

incorporation into learning (Singapore example), 59–60

testing students

controversies regarding tests in public education, 129–132

dark side of data, 121

Toigo, Ron, 138–140

Tomlinson, Sir Mike, 80–81

touch-screen technology, 47, 65

Tower Hamlets

conditions in East End of London and, 106–108

linking to parallel research to PBE study, 180

"prodigal leadership" process, 150

project in East End, 108–111

success based on foundations previously established, 149

use of case studies in PBE study, 178

tradition. see heritage

transparency, in use of metrics, 172–173

trial and error approach, in applying creativity and innovation, 168

trust, building, 170–171

Twitter

Burberry's use of social media, 63

Shoebuy.com use of social media, 127

U

uplift, defined, 1–2

uplifting actions. see journey to higher performance

uplifting leadership, introduction collaboration with competition, 12

uplifting leadership, introduction
(cont'd)
creativity and counter-flow, 11–12
dreaming with determination,
10–11
emotional and spiritual, 2–4
investigation of factors in, 6–7
journey to higher performance,
14–16
meaningful measurements,
13–14
performance and results, 4–6
push/pull approach, 12–13
social and community, 4
sustainable success, 14
turning failure into success, 1–2
what uplifting leadership
is, 9–10
what uplifting leadership is not,
7–9
US women's soccer team example, of
dreaming and believing, 23

V
Vancouver Giants hockey team
example of sustainable success,
138–140

expanding the audience of the PBE
study, 179
use of case studies in PBE
study, 178
vision
bringing back core vision to
Burberry, 64
collective identity derived from
common dream, 19
Vogel, Dean, 26, 28–31

W
weaknesses, converting into
strengths, 171
Weber, Max, 161
Weick, Karl, 155
welfare, knowing/being
concerned with your people's
welfare, 170
women's sports, US women's soccer
team impact on, 23

Z
*Zen and the Art of Motor Cycle
Maintenance* (Pirsig), 164
zero-sum games, competition and
collaboration and, 76